Our American Century

★

Turbulent Years · The 60s

★

By the Editors of Time-Life Books, Alexandria, Virginia

With a Foreword by Richard B. Stolley

Contents

★

Foreword

The haunting image at right freezes a moment that would never return: An hour later, the handsome president was dead, the governor badly wounded, and the beautiful woman in pink the most famous widow in the world. And the 1960s were only a third gone. Still ahead: tragic casualties in Vietnam, ruined political careers, civil rights violence, student rage. Turbulent years, indeed.

Through luck and *Life* magazine, where I was bureau chief in Los Angeles, Washington, and Paris, I was an eyewitness to many of the

events that rocked the decade. I arrived in Dallas a few hours after the assassination, and thanks to a cop's tip, obtained the celebrated Zapruder home movie of Kennedy's murder for *Life* exclusively. Watching that six-second scrap of grisly film for the first time remains the most unforgettable moment of my career.

When the landmark 1964 Civil Rights Act passed the Senate, I sat in the press gallery and marveled that the Jim Crow laws that had almost gotten me killed in the South only a few years earlier had been swept into history. I visited Vietnam with President Johnson and heard him order victory with these prideful words to the troops: "Boys, I want you to nail that coonskin to the wall." Three years later he was a broken and disgraced man.

During the '60s I spent time with headliners like Muhammad Ali (gigantic and guileless), Bobby Kennedy (a frequently abrasive man), Elizabeth Taylor (the eyes are lavender beyond imagining), Wernher von Braun (possibly the smartest human being I ever met), Ronald Reagan (the most articulate actor in Hollywood, which may say more about Hollywood than the Gipper).

Among its distinctions, the '60s arguably inflicted more devastating blows on American society than any other decade of this century. We winced; we wept; but we weathered the turbulence. And in time we became, Hail Columbia, a happy land again.

Dick Stolley

During a civil rights campaign in Birmingham, Alabama, in May 1963, firemen blast demonstrators off their feet with an extremely high-pressure stream from a fire hose, bloodying some and knocking others unconscious.

Beatles Paul McCartney (far left), George Harrison, John Lennon, and Ringo Starr set their moptops shaking on the eve of their arrival in America in 1964. The charismatic foursome soon became the top rock stars of the decade.

Marines recover the body of a comrade killed in combat in Vietnam in 1966. On television and in print, a continual barrage of wrenching images like this one brought the trauma of the war to Americans back home.

An antiwar protester plants a symbol of peace in a military policeman's rifle during a demonstration at the Pentagon in 1967.

A kaleidoscopic light show and the high-decibel music of Procol Harum generate a hallucinatory spectacle at New York's Anderson Theater in 1968. Such dazzling sensory overloads came to define the psychedelic experience.

Flowers in their hair, folk singer Arlo Guthrie and his bride, Jackie, are serenaded by Judy Collins. A hero to a generation of idealists, Guthrie predicted, "People are simply gonna learn that they can get more by being groovy than greedy."

On July 20, 1969, Edwin "Buzz" Aldrin salutes the flag he and Neil Armstrong planted on the Moon. Seen on television by 600 million people worldwide, the first lunar landing gave Americans wearied by Vietnam something to cheer about.

Winds of Change: 1960-1969

The bright scenes from the beginning would linger in the nation's collective memory, as would the mournful images at the end. The late January sun, reflected from the new-fallen snow, cast everything in brilliant relief. The light was so blinding, in fact, that Robert Frost, the 86-year-old poet, could not see to read from his notes for the inaugural ceremony, so he recited the poem from memory.

John Fitzgerald Kennedy stepped forward to be sworn in as the 35th president of the United States. He was hatless despite the subfreezing cold, and he had removed his topcoat for the ceremony. He was, at 43, the youngest person ever elected to lead the nation, and the first Catholic as well. His predecessor, Dwight D. Eisenhower, standing nearby in topcoat and scarf, was 70 years old and the oldest chief executive in U.S. history. "Let the word go forth," Kennedy declared in his inaugural address, "from this time and place, to friend and foe alike, that the torch has been passed to a new generation of Americans."

The youthful vigor of Kennedy's inauguration in 1961—with his summons to "pay any price, bear any burden, meet any hardship, to assure the survival and the success of liberty"—seemed to signal the dawn of a new era of American power and idealism. Kennedy established the Peace Corps, supported a tragic invasion of Cuban exiles at the Bay of Pigs, brought the world to the brink of nuclear war in a successful showdown over Soviet missiles in Cuba, and committed the United States to land men on the Moon. Then, after less than three years in office and before his early promise could be fulfilled, he was gone—the first of the leaders of the '60s to fall to an assassin's bullet.

Nearly four years before, at the very dawn of the new decade, one of the scholars Kennedy would recruit for his administration, the historian Arthur Schlesinger Jr., had ventured a prediction. "The Sixties," he wrote in January 1960, "will probably be spirited, articulate, inventive, incoherent, turbulent, with energy shooting off wildly in all directions." The decade became all of that and more. No 10-year period since the Civil

A Timeline of the 60s

1960

Four African Americans *stage a sit-in at Woolworth's whites-only lunch counter in Greensboro, N.C.*

The first Playboy Club *opens in Chicago.*

An American U-2 *high-altitude reconnaissance plane is shot down over Soviet territory, and the pilot, Lieutenant Francis Gary Powers, is captured.*

The first birth-control pill, *Enovid, is approved by the Federal Drug Administration.*

The laser *(Light Amplification by Stimulated Emission of Radiation) is first demonstrated by its inventor, Theodore Maimen.*

Gold-medal winners *at the summer Olympics in Rome include Cassius Clay, light-heavyweight boxing; Rafer Johnson, decathlon; and Wilma Rudolph, the first American woman to collect three gold medals in track and field.*

Richard M. Nixon *and John F. Kennedy, the Republican and Democratic candidates for the presidency, engage in the first of four televised campaign issue debates.*

CPR, *a method of saving heart-attack victims, is demonstrated at Johns Hopkins Hospital in Baltimore, Maryland.*

A new dance craze *sweeps the nation after Ernest "Chubby Checker" Evans dances and sings "The Twist" on "American Bandstand."*

John Fitzgerald Kennedy *is elected president by just over 100,000 votes, the narrowest margin since 1884.*

New on TV: *"The Flintstones"; "My Three Sons"; "The Andy Griffith Show"; "The Bob Newhart Show."*

New in print: *John Updike's "Rabbit, Run"; Harper Lee's "To Kill a Mockingbird"; Joy Adamson's "Born Free"; Bill Keane's cartoon "Family Circus."*

New products: *the felt-tip pen; AstroTurf; canned Coca-Cola; Lycra, a spandex fiber.*

The Academy Awards: *best picture—"The Apartment"; best actor—Burt Lancaster for "Elmer Gantry"; best actress—Elizabeth Taylor for "Butterfield 8."*

1961

The U.S. breaks diplomatic ties with Cuba *when its premier, Fidel Castro, accuses the U.S. of plotting military aggression against Cuba.*

The Peace Corps, *a volunteer program through which young Americans serve as goodwill ambassadors in underdeveloped nations, is created.*

Cosmonaut Yuri Gagarin *becomes the first human to orbit the earth.*

Four hundred anti-Communist Cuban exiles *die during the failed U.S. Bay of Pigs invasion intended to overthrow the government of Fidel Castro.*

Freedom Riders, *busloads of black and white civil rights workers, travel through the South in an effort to push the Kennedy administration to enforce the federal law prohibiting discrimination in interstate bus travel.*

Alan Shepard *makes the first U.S. manned spaceflight aboard Freedom 7.*

Ernest Hemingway, *Nobel Prize-winning novelist, dies of a self-inflicted gunshot wound*

East Germany *begins building the Berlin Wall, closing its borders with West Berlin.*

Roger Maris *hits 61 home runs in a single season, breaking Babe Ruth's record. However, Maris's season had 162 games as opposed to Ruth's 154-game season.*

The U.S. provides *the first direct military support to South Vietnam: 36 army helicopters and air and ground crews totaling nearly 400 men.*

New on TV: *"The Dick Van Dyke Show"; "Wide World of Sports"; "Car 54, Where Are You?"*

War was attended by such upheaval—by assassinations, political protest, war, cultural ferment, riots, and other turmoil.

Greater Expectations. The '60s appeared all the more tumultuous in contrast with the evident quiet of the decade that preceded. But underneath the placid surface of the 1950s the storm already had been gathering. The U.S. Supreme Court outlawed segregation in the public schools. In Montgomery, Alabama, a young Baptist minister named Martin Luther King Jr. demonstrated the power of nonviolent protest by leading a boycott of public buses. In Southeast Asia, a civil war was being fought in Vietnam. Millions of teenage Americans were dancing to the subversive beat of a new music called rock and roll.

The most crucial legacy from the '50s, however, was the wave of unparalleled national prosperity that spilled over and surged right through the new decade. The longest economic boom to date in U.S. history, it increased real per capita income by 41 percent during the '60s. This new affluence coincided with the impact of the bumper crop of post-World War II baby boomers coming of age. Much of this new generation grew up not only with more money, possessions, and educational opportunities than their forebears had had but also with greater expectations for themselves and their society.

A sense of hope and infectious optimism pervaded the middle class, especially the affluent young. Many felt that "the United States could have it all and do it all," observed the historian James Patterson, "that there were no limits to how comfortable and powerful and healthy and happy Americans could be." They also felt that they could make others happier at home and abroad, by attacking racial injustice and economic inequality and—in John Kennedy's hopeful words—assuring "the survival and the success of liberty."

Attacking Jim Crow. The struggle for equal rights was central to the '60s. The affluence of white America dramatized the plight of southern blacks, many of whom could not even vote. From the beginning of the decade the assault on Jim Crow was mounted head-on. Blacks and their white sympathizers deliberately broke laws upholding white supremacy. They sat in at segregated lunch counters, rode in the front of the bus, and staged illegal marches against discriminatory voter laws.

New in print: *Joseph Heller's "Catch-22"; Henry Miller's "Tropic of Cancer"; James Baldwin's "Nobody Knows My Name"; John H. Griffin's "Black Like Me."*

New products: *IBM Selectric typewriter; Coffee-mate; Total cereal; electric toothbrush; Lego bricks.*

The Academy Awards: *best picture—"West Side Story"; best actor—Maximilian Schell for "Judgment at Nuremberg"; best actress—Sophia Loren for "Two Women."*

1962

Jackie Robinson *becomes the first African American to be inducted into the Baseball Hall of Fame.*

John Glenn *becomes the first American to orbit the earth, circling it three times.*

Wilt Chamberlain *scores 100 points in a single game, breaking his previous record of 78 and raising Philadelphia over New York 169-147.*

Century 21 Exposition, *the first world's fair to be held in the U.S. in more than 20 years, opens in Seattle. It features a monorail and the 607-foot-tall Space Needle, with a revolving restaurant.*

The Supreme Court *bans* official *prayer in public schools as a violation of the First Amendment guarantee against state establishment of religion.*

Marilyn Monroe, *36 years old, dies of an overdose of sleeping pills.*

Thalidomide, *a drug found to cause widespread birth defects, is kept off the U.S. market through the efforts of Dr. Frances O. Kelsey of the FDA.*

James Meredith, *a black air force veteran, succeeds in enrolling at the University of Mississippi after being turned away three times. He begins classes under the protection of Justice Department officers.*

The Cuban missile crisis *erupts after the Soviet Union installs missile bases on the island, prompting President Kennedy to announce an air and sea quarantine of Cuba. After a six-day standoff, Khrushchev agrees to remove the missiles and dismantle the bases.*

New on TV: *"The Tonight Show Starring Johnny Carson"; "The Beverly Hillbillies"; "McHale's Navy"; "The Merv Griffin Show."*

New products: *Polaroid color film; The Easy Bake oven for children; Sprite soda.*

New in print: *Ken Kesey's "One Flew Over the Cuckoo's Nest"; Rachel Carson's "Silent Spring"; Michael Harrington's "The Other America."*

The Academy Awards: *best picture—"Lawrence of Arabia"; best actor—Gregory Peck for "To Kill a Mockingbird"; best actress—Anne Bancroft for "The Miracle Worker."*

1963

Eugene "Bull" Connor, *commissioner of public safety in Birmingham, Alabama, turns dogs and fire hoses on civil rights demonstrators.*

Pope John XXIII, *considered the most influential pope of this century, dies at age 81.*

Alabama governor *George Wallace defies a court order and refuses to allow two black students to enroll at the University of Alabama.*

Medgar Evers, *a field secretary for the NAACP, is gunned down outside his home in Jackson, Mississippi.*

A Partial Test Ban Treaty, *which bans nuclear tests in the ocean, the atmosphere, and space, is signed by the U.S., the U.S.S.R., and Great Britain.*

The five-digit zip code *is adopted by the U.S. Post Office to speed up mail sorting.*

Martin Luther King Jr. *gives his "I Have a Dream" speech at the March on Washington for jobs and freedom.*

A hotline *between Moscow and Washington is opened to reduce communication delays that might lead to an accidental nuclear war.*

Their actions brought retribution. In Mississippi, civil rights workers were murdered. In Birmingham, black children faced high-pressure fire hoses and attack dogs. In Selma, marchers protesting Jim Crow voting practices were clubbed and kicked by the very public authorities who were supposed to protect them. But the demonstrators did not fight back. Adhering to the Gandhian principles of nonviolence, they offered only passive resistance.

This astonished a nation accustomed to the tradition of self-defense —and galvanized its conscience. In 1963, more than 250,000 people from a wide spectrum of backgrounds converged on the nation's capital for the March on Washington. This was the occasion for Martin Luther King to describe his dream of a just society, one in which his four children would be judged "not by the color of their skin but by the content of their character."

Historic legislation followed. President Lyndon B. Johnson, Kennedy's successor, in 1964 pushed through the Congress the most significant civil rights legislation since Reconstruction, outlawing discrimination in employment and public accommodations. The following year, he won approval of the Voting Rights Act to ensure justice at the ballot box. In his nationally televised address proposing this measure, Johnson brought tears to King's eyes by echoing in his deep Texas drawl the movement's stirring anthem—"We shall overcome."

The Rights Revolution. The struggle in the South helped set the pattern for further attacks on the status quo. Its idealism and courage inspired the creation of other movements born of rising expectations and devoted to the enforcement of existing rights or the expansion of new ones.

Young people constituted a significant force for change. Thanks to the baby boom, the number of Americans aged 15 through 24 grew by nearly half during the '60s, accounting for more than one-sixth of the population by the end of the decade. College enrollment nearly doubled during the decade. In 1964, the Free Speech Movement paralyzed the University of California at Berkeley in protest against what its student leader, Mario Savio, called "depersonalized, unresponsive bureaucracy."

Students at many colleges began to demand a say in curriculum, regulations, and the larger society. Encouraged by the Students for a Democratic Society and other organizations of the so-called New Left, the feel-

Four black girls *are killed and another 22 adults and children are injured when a bomb explodes in a Birmingham, Alabama, church just before Sunday services. A Ku Klux Klan member is later convicted of the murders.*

A political coup in South Vietnam *backed by the U.S. overthrows the regime of Ngo Dinh Diem, who along with his brother is murdered.*

President John F. Kennedy is assassinated *in Dallas, Texas. Lyndon B. Johnson takes the oath of office 99 minutes later aboard Air Force One.*

Lee Harvey Oswald, *the man accused in the assassination of President Kennedy, is shot to death by Jack Ruby in the basement of police headquarters in Dallas as millions of people watch on television.*

New on TV: *"Let's Make a Deal"; "General Hospital"; "My Favorite Martian"; "Petticoat Junction."*

New in print: *Sylvia Plath's "The Bell Jar"; Kurt Vonnegut's "Cat's Cradle"; Betty Friedan's "The Feminine Mystique."*

New products: *Trimline phone; pushbutton phone; boil-in-the-bag vegetables from Green Giant.*

The Academy Awards: *best picture—"Tom Jones"; best actor—Sidney Poitier for "Lilies of the Field"; best actress—Patricia Neal for "Hud."*

1964

The Beatles visit America, *performing on "The Ed Sullivan Show" and at Carnegie Hall.*

Cassius Clay *beats Sonny Liston in seven rounds to win the heavyweight championship.*

Three civil rights workers, *James Chaney, Michael Schwerner, and Andrew Goodman, are murdered in Mississippi during the Freedom Summer voting rights drive.*

The Civil Rights Act of 1964 *is passed by Congress. It prohibits discrimination on the basis of race in employment, public accommodations, publicly owned facilities, union membership, and federally funded programs.*

U.S. aircraft bomb *North Vietnamese gunboat bases as a reprisal for an alleged attack on U.S. destroyers in the Gulf of Tonkin.*

Nikita Khrushchev is ousted *as first secretary of the Communist Party and is replaced by Leonid Brezhnev. Aleksei Kosygin becomes the premier.*

President Lyndon Johnson *is reelected over Barry Goldwater in a landslide victory of 43 million to 27 million votes.*

The Nobel Peace Prize *is awarded to Dr. Martin Luther King Jr. for his nonviolent resistance to racial oppression.*

Silicone gel sacs *for breast implants are first used in plastic surgery.*

New on TV: *"Jeopardy"; "Bewitched"; "Gilligan's Island"; "The Munsters"; "Flipper"; "The Addams Family."*

New products: *Ford Mustang; Kellog's Pop-Tarts; Diet Pepsi.*

New in print: *Marshall McLuhan's "Understanding Media: The Extensions of Man"; Saul Bellow's "Herzog"; Timothy Leary's "The Psychedelic Experience"; Joanne Greenberg's "I Never Promised You a Rose Garden."*

The Academy Awards: *best picture—"My Fair Lady"; best actor—Rex Harrison for "My Fair Lady"; best actress—Julie Andrews for "Mary Poppins."*

1965

Winston Churchill *dies at age 90.*

Malcolm X *is assassinated at a rally in Harlem.*

A 50-mile march for freedom *from Selma to Montgomery, Alabama, by civil rights demonstrators is led by Dr. Martin Luther King Jr.*

The first American combat troops *in South Vietnam land at Da Nang in March.*

Gemini 3, *with astronauts John Young and Gus Grissom aboard, kicks off NASA's two-man Gemini space program.*

The Medicare bill, *expanding Social Security programs to provide a variety of medical services, is signed into law.*

"Burn, baby, burn" *echoes in the Watts section of Los Angeles when a clash between blacks and white police officers escalates into a five-day riot.*

Draft-card burning *is declared a crime by Congress.*

ing grew among the young that American life had to be transformed—
and that only they could do it.

Folk songs, rock and roll lyrics, and an upsurge of satirical comedy
known as black humor helped shape the rebellious moral vision of the
young. In the nightclubs, comedians Lenny Bruce, Mort Sahl, and Dick
Gregory broke new political ground. Works like Stanley Kubrick's film
Dr. Strangelove or: How I Learned to Stop Worrying and Love the Bomb
ridiculed the excesses of the Cold War. Joseph Heller's book *Catch-22*
vividly caught the insanity of bureaucracy gone amuck.

Dropping Out. Many of the young opted out of the mainstream and
tried to create a "counterculture" of their own. Rock was their marching
music, "doing your own thing" their motto. In the bohemian tradition,
these hippies, as they were called, wore their hair long, exulted in poetry,
and adopted flowers as their symbol. They smoked marijuana openly,
sometimes experimented with hallucinogens and harder drugs, advocated free sexual relationships, and reached out for wisdom from Eastern
religions. Some founded communes hoping to discover in their own
utopias the sense of personal intimacy and authenticity they missed in
mainstream America.

The Women's Movement. The long-dormant feminist movement was
jolted into action in 1963 by Betty Friedan's bestseller *The Feminine
Mystique,* a powerful exploration of the high personal and social costs of
confining women to the traditional roles of wife and mother. In some
ways feminism—"women's lib," in '60s shorthand—shocked Americans
more than did the movement for black equality. Even among civil
rights workers, student protesters, and members of the counterculture,
woman's "place" was understood to be in helping men. In 1966 Friedan
cofounded the National Organization for Women (NOW), which led the
battle against "Jane Crow" for equal employment opportunities, equal
pay for equal work, and liberalization of abortion laws.

At the local level, meanwhile, women in "consciousness raising"
groups met to share their experiences of a male-dominated world. Many
men feared that women's liberation threatened the very existence of
marriage and family, and the battle of the sexes became one more struggle polarizing American society.

Sandy Koufax *of the Los Angeles Dodgers throws a perfect game against the Chicago Cubs, becoming the first major-league pitcher to win four no-hitters.*

Caesar Chavez, *founder of the National Farm Workers Association (NFWA), takes his small union out on strike in a show of solidarity for grape pickers in California seeking better wages and working conditions.*

A massive blackout *in New York City, six states, and parts of Canada leaves 30 million people without electricity.*

New on TV: *"Days of Our Lives"; "Green Acres"; "Get Smart"; "I Dream of Jeannie"; "Hogan's Heroes."*

New products: *Apple Jacks cereal; Gatorade; SpaghettiOs.*

New in print: *Tom Wolfe's "The Kandy-Colored, Tangerine-Flake Stream-Line Baby"; Timothy Leary's "The Psychedelic Reader"; Ralph Nader's "Unsafe at Any Speed"; "Autobiography of Malcolm X."*

The Academy Awards: *best picture—"The Sound of Music"; best actor—Lee Marvin for "Cat Ballou"; best actress—Julie Christie for "Darling."*

1966

Cigarette packages *begin carrying a printed warning from the U.S. Surgeon General: "Caution: Cigarette smoking may be hazardous to your health."*

The Supreme Court rules *in the Miranda case that criminals must be advised of their rights upon arrest.*

The National Organization for Women (NOW) *is formed. Betty Friedan is one of its founders.*

Eight student nurses *are stabbed and strangled by drifter Richard Speck. He is sentenced to 600 years in prison.*

Charles Whitman, *a student at the University of Texas, shoots 44 people from a 307-foot tower on campus, killing 13 of them before he himself is killed by police.*

The Black Panther Party, *whose manifesto calls for "power to determine the destiny of our black community," is founded in Oakland, California, by Huey Newton (above, right) and Bobby Seale (left).*

Roman Catholic bishops *rule that American Catholics are no longer required to abstain from eating meat on Fridays except during Lent.*

New on TV: *"The Newlywed Game"; "Mission: Impossible"; "The Hollywood Squares"; "Batman"; "Star Trek"; "The Monkees"; "The Dating Game."*

New products: *Taster's Choice freeze-dried instant coffee; Bac*Os*

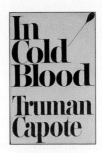

New in print: *Truman Capote's "In Cold Blood"; Jean Nidetch's "Weight Watchers Cookbook"; Jacqueline Susann's "The Valley of the Dolls."*

The Academy Awards: *best picture—"A Man for All Seasons"; best actor—Paul Scofield for "A Man for All Seasons"; best actress— Elizabeth Taylor for "Who's Afraid of Virginia Woolf?"*

1967

The first "Human Be-In" *is celebrated as some 20,000 hippies jam Golden Gate Park in San Francisco.*

In the first Super Bowl *the Green Bay Packers, led by quarterback Bart Starr, beat the Kansas City Chiefs 35-10.*

War and Antiwar. The issue that would overshadow all of the decade's discord erupted during the second half of the '60s. United States involvement in Vietnam had begun gradually with the commitment of advisers by Eisenhower and then Kennedy. Then, in 1965, Johnson sent combat troops to South Vietnam and began bombing the North. The war became the longest and most unpopular conflict in U.S. history, and it intensified the splintering of U.S. society. Many students turned against the war because of the draft or because they considered it wrong. They staged teach-ins and then moved on to marches, sit-ins, and other forms of protest borrowed from the civil rights battle. Vietnam widened the gap between generations as many older, more conservative citizens labeled the young anti-American and the young cautioned against trusting anyone over 30.

Among those of the older generation who bridged the gap was the best-known pediatrician in America, Dr. Benjamin Spock, who was well into his sixties. Most of Spock's young fellow war protesters had been reared by the gentle dictates of his best-selling *Baby and Child Care*. Published in 1946 near the onset of the baby boom, his book countered traditional manuals that advised parents against holding or kissing the baby. "Trust yourself," Spock told parents. "You know more than you think you do." His compassionate counsel led some critics to hold Spock accountable for the antiauthoritarianism of the new generation.

Spock was one of many who suffered from the growing '60s backlash. A lot of Americans were angry and fearful about long-haired hippies, campus rebellions, the casual new sexual code, and, above all, opposition to the war. In such an atmosphere the famous baby doctor was convicted of conspiring against the draft and sentenced to two years in prison—a decision overturned on appeal.

The Violent Years. As the fighting in Vietnam escalated, the level of turmoil and outright violence rose at home. The focus of the civil rights movement shifted northward to the urban ghettos, where deep-rooted poverty and social despair proved less susceptible to the tactics of passive resistance. Militant new voices were heard. Black Power and black separatism became the new rallying cries, drowning out the drive toward racial integration. "Violence," declared one young firebrand, H. Rap Brown, was "as American as apple pie." Riots born of frustration and

Apollo 1 astronauts *Roger Chaffee, Virgil Grissom, and Edward White die when a flash fire breaks out in their spacecraft during ground testing.*

Elvis Presley *marries Priscilla Beaulieu in Las Vegas.*

State laws against interracial marriage *are ruled unconstitutional by the Supreme Court.*

Thurgood Marshall *becomes the first African American appointed to the Supreme Court.*

Billie Jean King *wins the U.S. Open, completing her sweep of American and British women's singles, doubles, and mixed doubles tennis championships.*

Antiwar demonstrators, *estimated at 150,000, gather at the Lincoln Memorial in Washington, D.C., to protest U.S. policy in Vietnam.*

Dr. Christiaan Barnard *performs the first heart transplant in Cape Town, South Africa.*

Lynda Bird Johnson, *the president's daughter, weds marine captain Charles Robb in a ceremony at the White House.*

The first supersonic airliner, *the Concorde, is unveiled by Britain and France.*

New on TV: *"The Flying Nun"; "The Carol Burnett Show"; "The Smothers Brothers Comedy Hour"; "The Phil Donahue Show"; "Ironside."*

New products: *Peter Max-designed posters, decals, and clothing; Fresca soda; Amana commercial microwave ovens; the Chevrolet Camaro.*

New in print: *Marshall McLuhan's "The Medium Is the Message"; Jonathan Kozol's "Death at an Early Age"; Sue Kaufmann's "Diary of a Mad Housewife"; "Rolling Stone" magazine.*

The Academy Awards: *best picture—"In the Heat of the Night"; best actor—Rod Steiger for "In the Heat of the Night"; best actress—Katharine Hepburn for "Guess Who's Coming to Dinner?"*

1968

The success of the Communist Tet offensive *in South Vietnam stuns the American military leadership and the public.*

The USS Pueblo, *a navy spy ship, is seized by North Korean gunboats in international waters. The ship is impounded and its crew of 83 are kept prisoner for nearly a year.*

New York senator Robert F. Kennedy *becomes a candidate for the Democratic presidential nomination in March.*

Race riots *erupt across America after Dr. Martin Luther King, in Memphis to support striking sanitation workers, is assassinated.*

The Civil Rights Act of 1968, *which includes a fair-housing provision and protection of civil rights workers from intimidation or injury, is signed by President Johnson.*

Students at Columbia University *take over campus buildings to protest the university's involvement with the Pentagon-funded Institute for Defense Analysis as well as the school's plans to build a new gymnasium in a location where low-income housing is needed.*

Peace talks begin in Paris *between the U.S., led by ambassador-at-large W. Averell Harriman, and North Vietnam.*

Robert F. Kennedy, *having won the California Democratic primary, is assassinated at the Ambassador Hotel in downtown Los Angeles. Sirhan Sirhan is arrested and is later convicted of first-degree murder.*

hopelessness racked dozens of U.S. cities. Entire sections of urban ghettos were burned out and looted, and scores of people died—almost all of them black.

The turmoil, both foreign and domestic, peaked in 1968 as critical events followed one another in quick succession. In January, Communists in South Vietnam mounted the Tet offensive, a countrywide assault that failed militarily but succeeded politically by undermining official U.S. claims of "light at the end of the tunnel." In March, President Johnson, his credibility crumbling, announced that he would not seek reelection. In April, Martin Luther King was assassinated in Memphis, triggering riots in more than 130 cities. In June, Senator Robert Kennedy, seeking the Democratic presidential nomination, died of an assassin's bullet in Los Angeles. In August, youthful protesters in Chicago, attempting to disrupt the streets outside the Democratic National Convention where Hubert Humphrey was being nominated, were violently assaulted by the police. In November, Richard M. Nixon, who had narrowly lost to Jack Kennedy at the beginning of the decade and now appealed to what he called "the silent majority," was elected president.

Rising Above It. The tumult of the '60s was emotionally amplified because much of it came into the living room via television. By the end of the decade practically every household in America contained at least one TV set and thus resided electronically in "the global village," as the Canadian-born media theorist Marshall McLuhan described it. Americans could vicariously empathize with protesters being beaten at Selma, grieve along with the widows Jacqueline Kennedy and Coretta King, witness in disbelief the killing of the accused assassin Lee Harvey Oswald by Jack Ruby, and recoil from the carnage in Vietnam.

This medium that so embroiled Americans in the turbulence of the '60s also enabled them to briefly rise above it all. Since 1961, when President Kennedy committed the nation to go to the Moon, the astronauts—a heroic corps of men with short hair—had completed 20 space missions of increasing complexity. Their adventure culminated with the success of *Apollo 11* on July 20, 1969. In that transcendent moment when Neil Armstrong stepped onto the lunar surface 241,580 miles away, more than half a billion people were watching from their troubled planet back home.

James Earl Ray *is charged with the assassination of Martin Luther King Jr.*

During the Democratic National Convention *in Chicago, a riot leaves more than 1,000 student protesters, antiwar demonstrators, and bystanders injured by police.*

The Miss America Pageant *is picketed by members of the National Women's Liberation Party, which denounces the annual pageant as degrading to women.*

Arthur Ashe *wins the U.S. Open, becoming the first African American male to win a major tennis tournament.*

Abbie Hoffman, *leader of the Yippies (Youth International Party), is arrested for wearing a shirt that resembles the American flag. He is charged under a federal law making it a crime to cast contempt upon the flag.*

Jacqueline Kennedy *marries Greek shipping businessman Aristotle Onassis on the island of Skorpios.*

Olympians Tommie Smith and John Carlos, *the gold- and bronze-medal winners in the 200-meter race in Mexico City, raise their fists in a Black Power salute as the U.S. national anthem is played.*

New on TV: *"Rowan and Martin's Laugh-In"; "Hawaii Five-O"; "60 Minutes"; "The Mod Squad"; "Julia."*

New products: *McDonald's Big Mac; waterbeds; Jacuzzi whirlpool baths.*

New in print: *Eldridge Cleaver's "Soul on Ice"; Tom Wolfe's "The Electric Kool-Aid Acid Test"; Arthur C. Clarke's "2001: A Space Odyssey."*

The Academy Awards: *best picture—"Oliver!"; best actor—Cliff Robertson for "Charly"; best actress—Katharine Hepburn for "The Lion in Winter" and Barbra Streisand for "Funny Girl."*

1969

Richard M. Nixon, *sworn in as the 37th president of the United States, calls for peace in Vietnam in his inaugural address.*

The "Saturday Evening Post," *founded in 1821, publishes its last issue on February 8.*

Joe Namath *and his underdog New York Jets teammates beat the Baltimore Colts to become the first AFL Super Bowl winners.*

Dwight D. Eisenhower, *World War II hero and former U.S. president, dies at age 78.*

The German measles (rubella) *vaccine becomes available in the U.S.*

Senator Edward Kennedy *drives his car off a bridge on Chappaquiddick Island in Massachusetts. A passenger, Mary Jo Kopechne, dies in the accident.*

The Eagle, *Apollo 11's lunar module, lands on the Moon.*

Cult leader Charles Manson *and his followers are charged with the murder of actress Sharon Tate, wife of film director Roman Polanski, and six others.*

Woodstock, *an open-air music festival, attracts 400,000 people and features performers such as the Who, Janis Joplin, Jimi Hendrix, and the Grateful Dead.*

The Chicago Seven, *including Abbie Hoffman, Tom Hayden, Jerry Rubin, and Bobby Seale, go on trial on charges of conspiring to incite a riot during the 1968 Democratic convention.*

The New York Mets *beat the Baltimore Orioles to win their first World Series.*

The U.S. and the U.S.S.R. *meet for the first time in Helsinki for the Strategic Arms Limitation Treaty (SALT) talks to seek an end to the nuclear arms race.*

New on TV: *"The Brady Bunch"; "The Bill Cosby Show"; "Hee Haw"; "Marcus Welby, M.D."; Sesame Street (with the Jim Henson Muppets).*

New in print: *Kurt Vonnegut's "Slaughterhouse Five"; Maya Angelou's "I Know Why the Caged Bird Sings"; Elizabeth Kubler-Ross's "On Death and Dying"; "Penthouse" magazine.*

New products: *Frosted Mini-Wheats; Campbell's Chunky soups.*

The Academy Awards: *best picture—"Midnight Cowboy"; best actor—John Wayne for "True Grit"; best actress—Maggie Smith for "The Prime of Miss Jean Brodie."*

Voices From a Turbulent Decade

★

SEVEN WHO SHAPED THE 60S

When Bob Dylan warned in 1964 that "The Times They Are a-Changin'," he spoke for a collection of outspoken individuals who shaped the decade. Betty Friedan raised an impassioned cry for women's rights while Ralph Nader campaigned tirelessly for consumer rights. Malcolm X employed fiery rhetoric to deliver a wake-up call about race relations. Using a different idiom, Andy Warhol created images that spoke to the crass materialism of American culture.

But it was Dylan, born Robert Allen Zimmerman in Hibbing, Minnesota, whose gravelly, nasal voice best captured the spirit of a tumultuous decade. This shopkeeper's son took his new name from Welsh poet Dylan Thomas and his inspiration from everyone from folk singer Woody Guthrie to poet Allen Ginsberg. His biting musical poems like "Blowin' in the Wind" and "A Hard Rain's a-Gonna Fall" questioned Establishment values and lent an uncompromising sound to the '60s protest movement. Blending prophecy, parable, metaphor, and the whine of the harmonica, Dylan's anthems forged a link between popular music and political and social activism. "The teachers in school taught me everything was fine," Dylan mused. "But it ain't fine, man. There are so many lies that have been told, so many things that are kept back. Kids have a feeling like me, but they ain't hearing it no place. They're scared to step out. But I ain't scared to do it, man." Stepping out, Dylan inspired a generation to do the same.

Rumpled and unshaven, 22-year-old Bob Dylan takes a drag on his cigarette. "I come on stage the same way I go anywhere," he said. "I mean, all these people are paying me to look neat?"

A Vision for Society

L yndon Johnson was often compared unfavorably with his polished predecessor John Kennedy, especially by the eastern Establishment. Johnson was rough hewn, earthy, often crude. He was also a master politician, as even his detractors had to admit. As soon as Johnson stepped into the presidential shoes, he began jump-starting some stalled items on the social agenda he inherited from Kennedy. Expansive and optimistic, he said, "Hell, we're the richest country in the world, the most powerful. We can do it all." Wheeling, dealing, bullying, and cajoling, Johnson pushed two landmark civil rights bills through Congress, in 1964 and 1965. As civil rights leader Julian Bond observed, the president "fought against his regionalism, fought against the parochialism . . . he had been raised in, and became a truly national leader." He oversaw the birth of Medicare and described a "Great Society" that, he predicted, would conquer poverty.

Johnson's campaign for social progress hit its high point in 1965, then began to founder as he relentlessly escalated the war in Vietnam. The master politician had miscalculated: Even the richest and most powerful nation in the world could not do it all.

No memorial or oration or eulogy could more eloquently honor President Kennedy's memory than the earliest possible passage of the civil rights bill for which he fought so long. We have talked long enough about equal rights in this country. We have talked for one hundred years or more. It is time now to write the next chapter and write it in the books of law.
—Speech to Congress, November 1963

This administration today, here and now, declares unconditional war on poverty in America.
—State of the Union address, January 1964

Let me say to every Negro in this country, you must register, you must vote. . . . The vote is the most powerful instrument ever devised by man for breaking down injustice.
—Speech at the signing of the 1965 Voting Rights Act

Lyndon Johnson plays cowboy with grandson Patrick Lyndon Nugent in June 1968. Six months later, his political career shattered by Vietnam, he retreated to Texas.

From *The Feminine Mystique*:

It was a strange stirring, a sense of dissatisfaction, a yearning that women suffered in the middle of the twentieth century in the United States. Each suburban wife struggled with it alone. As she made the beds, shopped for groceries, matched slipcover material, ate peanut butter sandwiches with her children, chauffeured Cub Scouts and Brownies, lay beside her husband at night—she was afraid to ask even of herself the silent question—"Is this all?"

It is my thesis that the core of the problem for women today is not sexual but a problem of identity—a stunting or evasion of growth that is perpetuated by the feminine mystique. . . . Our culture does not permit women to accept or gratify their basic need to grow and fulfill their potentialities as human beings, a need which is not solely defined by their sexual role.

The mystique spelled out a choice—love, home, children, or other goals and purposes in life. Given such a choice, was it any wonder that so many American women chose love as their whole purpose?

Men fell for the mystique without a murmur of dissent.

Our society forces boys, insofar as it can, to grow up. . . . Why aren't girls forced to grow up—to achieve somehow the core of self that will end the unnecessary dilemma, the mistaken choice between femaleness and humanness that is implied in the feminine mystique?

If a job is to be the way out of a trap for a woman, it must be a job that she can take seriously as part of a life plan.

Feminism Reborn

As the 15th reunion of Smith College's class of 1942 approached, Betty Friedan agreed to carry out a survey of her classmates and report on what they had been doing since graduating in 1942. Friedan, a suburban wife, mother of three, and freelance journalist, was startled at the deep undercurrent of malaise in her classmates' responses. They had accepted the domestic role that the ideal woman was supposed to play in postwar America, and had found that it wasn't enough. "I'm B.J.'s wife; I'm Jenny's mother," one woman wrote, "but who am I?" Said another, "The problem is always being the children's mommy or the minister's wife and never being myself."

Friedan, who had once turned down a fellowship to study at Berkeley because her boyfriend warned that it could end their relationship (she complied with his wishes and the relationship ended anyway), distilled her classmates' experiences into a magazine article. All of the women's magazines that had previously published her work turned it down, and an editor for *Redbook* told her, "Only the most neurotic housewife would identify with this."

Refusing to be discouraged, she sold the idea to a book publisher, and in 1963 *The Feminine Mystique* appeared. In it she exposed what she called "the problem that has no name": that in seeking fulfillment exclusively through their homes and families, women had lost their own identities. "If we continue to produce millions of young mothers who stop their growth and education short of identity, without a strong core of human values to pass on to their children," Friedan warned, "we are committing, quite simply, genocide."

After publishing her call to arms in 1966, Friedan helped found the National Organization for Women (NOW). *The Feminine Mystique*, NOW, and Friedan herself powered the decade's drive for full equality for women.

Betty Friedan, who was fired from her job after becoming pregnant with her second child, denounced suburbia as "a bedroom and kitchen sexual ghetto."

*I was marked. I had a big head, and I looked
like Joe Louis in my cradle. People said so.
One day I threw my first punch and hit my
mother right in the teeth and knocked one
out. If you don't believe me, ask her.*

*This is a story about a man
With iron fists and a beautiful tan.
He talks a lot and he boasts indeed
Of a powerful punch and blinding speed.*

*They all must fall
In the round I call.*

*Some got mad
And some lost money
When I ripped home that right
As sweet as honey.*

*I am the greatest. I am the prettiest. I am so
pretty that I can hardly stand to look at myself. I am the fastest. I am the fastest heavyweight that you ever did see. Next to me,
Liston will look like a dump truck.*

*My secret is self-confidence, a champion
   at birth.
I'm lyrical, I'm fresh, I'm smart,
My fists have proved my worth.*

*Marcellus vanquished Carthage,
Cassius laid Julius Caesar low,
And Clay will flatten Douglas Jones
With a mighty, measured blow.*

*Float like a butterfly,
Sting like a bee.
His hands can't hit
What his eyes can't see.*

*God made us all, but some of us are made
special. . . . Some people have special
resources inside, and when God blesses you
to have more than others, you have a
responsibility to use it right.*

A Champ Like No Other

When Cassius Marcellus Clay Jr., the 22-year-old Olympic gold medalist from Louisville, Kentucky, entered the ring with heavyweight champion Sonny Liston on February 25, 1964, the Las Vegas bookies had set the odds against the baby-faced challenger at 8 to 1. All but three of the 46 ringside reporters anticipated a quick knockout by Liston, a fierce competitor who had felled his last three opponents in the first round. But this time the underdog prevailed, jabbing and dancing his way to victory in seven rounds. "Eat your words! Eat! Eat!" the new champion bellowed gleefully at the reporters.

Soon after his upset win, Clay announced that he was joining the Nation of Islam, a black-led religious group based in Chicago. The Black Muslims gave him a new name, Muhammad Ali, and they made him a minister. And he kept boxing, successfully defending his title against every challenger.

In 1967, when Ali was at the peak of his boxing career, he refused induction into the army on religious grounds. In resisting the draft he drove home a blow every bit as pointed and powerful as those he used to beat his opponents. "I ain't got no quarrel with those Vietcong," Ali explained. "They never called me nigger."

Convicted of draft dodging, he was sentenced to five years in jail and fined $10,000. The World Boxing Association revoked his title. Many fans, however, stood by their champ, who appealed. "They can take away the television cameras, the bright lights, the money, and ban you from the ring," a man in Chicago told Ali, "but they can't destroy your victory. You have taken a stand for the world and now you are the people's champion." Four years later, the U.S. Supreme Court vindicated Ali, voting unanimously to reverse his conviction.

"I'm the greatest!" crows Muhammad Ali. His manager said the boxer "could give Norman Vincent Peale lessons on the power of positive thinking."

Souper Man

Famed for declaring that in the future everyone would be famous for 15 minutes, Andy Warhol didn't have to settle for so short a span. He was a commercial artist in New York when in 1962 a friend suggested that he paint something so ordinary that nobody paid any attention to it—"something like a can of Campbell's soup."

That summer Warhol displayed 32 meticulous renderings of soup cans at a Los Angeles gallery. Detractors taunted the show (a neighboring gallery filled its windows with real cans of Campbell's soup, advertising them for 29 cents apiece), but the exhibit made him the hot new Pop artist. Back in New York, he used silkscreen and other mechanical processes to turn out images of familiar commodities, from Brillo boxes to Marilyn Monroe's face.

Some art critics called Warhol a fraud, while others saw in his work a commentary on the crass materialism of American society. Warhol was cryptic about what it meant, but he revealed that he liked mass-production techniques because he could have "somebody else do all my paintings for me."

Campbell's Soup Can I (Tomato), 1968

I never wanted to be a painter. I wanted to be a tap dancer.

If you want to know all about Andy Warhol, just look at the surface of my paintings and films and me, and there I am. There's nothing behind it.

If people never misunderstand you, and if they do everything exactly the way you tell them to, they're just transmitters of your ideas, and you get bored with that. But when you work with people who misunderstand you, instead of getting transmissions you get transmutations, and that's much more interesting in the long run.

I'd prefer to remain a mystery. I never like to give my background and, anyway, I make it all up different every time I'm asked.

I feel I'm very much a part of my times, of my culture, as much a part of it as rockets and television.

My paintings never turn out the way I expect them to, but I'm never surprised.

I want to be a machine. I think it would be terrific if everybody was alike.

I think every painting should be the same size and the same color so they're all interchangeable and nobody thinks they have a better painting or a worse painting.

In the future everybody will be world famous for fifteen minutes.

Once you "got" Pop, you could never see a sign the same way again. And once you thought Pop, you could never see America the same way again. . . . We were seeing the future and we knew it for sure. We saw people walking around in it without knowing it, because they were still thinking in the past, in the references of the past.

Buying is much more American than thinking.

Making money is art and working is art and good business is the best art.

Business art is the step that comes after art. I started as a commercial artist, and I want to finish as a business artist. After I did the thing called "art" or whatever it's called, I went into business art. I wanted to be an Art Businessman or Business Artist.

Thirty-nine-year-old Andy Warhol wears a wig to mask his baldness. "Andy," said an associate, "is a promoter who creates—and his greatest creation is himself."

A great problem of contemporary life is how to control the power of economic interests which ignore the harmful effects of their applied science and technology. . . . Our society's obligation to protect the "body rights" of its citizens with vigorous resolve and ample resources requires the precise, authoritative articulation and front-rank support which is being devoted to civil rights.

For over half a century the automobile has brought death, injury, and the most inestimable sorrow and deprivation to millions of people. With Medea-like intensity, this mass trauma began rising sharply four years ago, reflecting new and unexpected ravages by the motor vehicle. A 1959 Department of Commerce report projected that 51,000 persons would be killed by automobiles in 1975. That figure will probably be reached in 1965, a decade ahead of schedule.

There can be no daily democracy without daily citizenship.

I think a stake here in the whole consumer movement is not just the quality of the goods, not just honest pricing, which of course improves our allocation of resources, but also in my judgment the most critical area of all—an area which might be termed as the area of bodily rights. The right of one's physiological integrity from being invaded, assaulted or destroyed by the harmful by-products of industrial products and processing.

Manmade hazards are transcending our traditional physiological alert system. We can't taste the mercury in swordfish, we can't smell carbon dioxide, we can't see hydrocarbons or feel radioactivity from the nuclear plants. We've got to rely on our minds, less on our bodies, to signal pain or anger or fear. We have to do something.

The Consumer Evangelist

Ralph Nader came of age in an era in which what was good for General Motors was held to be good for the nation, but he didn't buy it. Moreover, he convinced consumers that they shouldn't either. In 1965 the 35-year-old Harvard Law School graduate published *Unsafe at Any Speed: The Designed-In Dangers of the American Automobile,* which lambasted the auto industry for sacrificing safety to improve profits. In particular, he accused General Motors of putting the Chevrolet Corvair on the road with a sloppily engineered rear-suspension system. The car was, Nader said, "one of the greatest acts of industrial irresponsibility in the present century."

Humiliated by the allegations, General Motors attempted to discredit Nader by hiring private detectives to investigate his politics, religion, and sex life. When word of the investigation leaked out, corporate executives were forced to apologize before a nationally televised Senate committee hearing. The resulting publicity as well as the $425,000 General Motors paid Nader to drop his invasion-of-privacy suit helped launch the consumer movement in America.

Lauded as the David who had battled the Goliath auto industry, Nader continued his fight for consumer rights by drawing national attention to the side effects of medical x-rays, the hazards of leaky natural-gas pipelines, the threat of radiation from certain color television sets, and unsafe practices in meat-processing plants. His tireless efforts not only generated public support for consumer rights but also led to the passage of such legislation as the Traffic and Motor Vehicle Safety Act of 1966 and the Wholesome Meat Act of 1967. Scores of idealistic staff members who joined the fight became known as Nader's Raiders. Transforming a nation of innocent shoppers into wary consumers, Nader proved that one man could make a difference.

A nonconsumer who wore the boots seen here for 20 years, Ralph Nader testifies in Washington before a House subcommittee on small business.

I believe in the brotherhood of man, all men, but I don't believe in brotherhood with anybody who doesn't want brotherhood with me.

If they make the Ku Klux Klan nonviolent, I'll be nonviolent. If they make the White Citizens' Council nonviolent, I'll be nonviolent. If the leaders of the nonviolent movement can go into the white community and teach nonviolence, good. I'd go along with that. But as long as I see them teaching nonviolence only in the Black community, then we can't go along with that.

I firmly believe that Negroes have the right to fight against these racists by any means that are necessary.

Yes, I'm an extremist. The black race here in North America is in extremely bad condition. You show me a black man who isn't an extremist and I'll show you one who needs psychiatric attention!

If you're born in America with a black skin, you're born in prison.

There can be no revolution without bloodshed, and it is nonsense to describe the civil rights movement in America as a revolution.

Revolution is bloody, revolution is hostile, revolution knows no compromise, revolution overturns and destroys everything that gets in its way.

Without education, you are not going anywhere in this world.

It's a time for martyrs now. And if I'm to be one, it will be in the cause of brotherhood. That's the only thing that can save this country. I've learned it the hard way—but I've learned it.

Black Power's Fiery Champion

In a decade shaped by angry blacks, Malcolm X called himself the angriest. While others campaigned for racial harmony, he advocated black power. "After 400 years of slave labor," he said, "we have some back pay coming."

Malcolm's childhood was scarred by the death of his father, a Baptist minister. The police called it an accident, but Malcolm believed that he had been killed by white supremacists. Several years later, his mother was committed to a mental institution. Turning first to petty thievery, then to drug dealing and burglary, Malcolm spent six years in prison. There he turned his life around, educating himself and becoming a member of the Nation of Islam. Like others in the group, he dropped his surname and substituted the letter *X* to mark the African family name that had been lost.

The Black Muslims, as they were known, believed in radical racial separatism. "Coffee is the only thing I like integrated," Malcolm once said wryly. He soon became their best-known spokesman, a charismatic advocate for his faith and a harsh judge of white America.

A pilgrimage to Mecca in 1964 led him to break with the Nation of Islam and start his own Islamic community. Though still committed to black nationalism, he grew more optimistic about prospects for change without bloodshed. "If the ballot doesn't work, we'll try something else," he said. "But let us try the ballot."

At a rally in Harlem the following year, just as he uttered the traditional Muslim greeting *As salaamu alaikum* ("Peace be unto you"), Malcolm was gunned down; three Nation of Islam loyalists were convicted of his murder. Dead at 39, he left a legacy of fierce racial pride and uncompromising principle that led African American actor Ossie Davis to eulogize him as "our manhood, our living, black manhood."

Malcolm X wears the symbol of Islam on his ring and a goatee. The beard was a sign of his break from the Nation of Islam, which strictly forbade facial hair.

A Brief Shining Moment

★

AMERICA VISITS CAMELOT

President John F. Kennedy took the oath of office during anxious times. Soviet-supported rebels were attempting takeovers in South Vietnam and Laos. Fidel Castro, Cuba's leader, was threatening to provide the Soviets with a beachhead only a short flight from Florida's coast. And the economy, once an engine of prosperity, had fallen into a slump.

Americans had felt a need for change, and, by a slim margin of 118,000, they had chosen the 43-year-old senator over Vice President Richard Nixon to bring it about. He seemed up to the task. Like the outgoing president, Dwight Eisenhower, Kennedy was a war hero. But he possessed some unique distinctions: He was the first Roman Catholic to serve as the nation's chief executive, a Pulitzer Prize-winning author, and the youngest man ever elected president. He and his stylish wife, Jacqueline, were the first White House occupants since Theodore Roosevelt to share the mansion with young children.

Kennedy suffered from back trouble so severe that he wore a canvas corset and habitually sought relief in his rocking chair *(inset)*, yet on Inauguration Day he radiated a youthful vigor that kindled idealism and hope for the future in what he called a new generation of Americans. "Ask not what your country can do for you," he implored them, "ask what you can do for your country."

John F. Kennedy announces the passing of the torch to a new generation as (from left to right in first row) Jackie Kennedy, former president Dwight Eisenhower, Lyndon Johnson, and Richard Nixon look on.

An Elegant White House

Part landmark, part national treasure, the White House has always been the nation's premier home. Yet when the Kennedys moved in, its interior looked shabby, and the rooms were furnished with department-store reproductions of antiques.

Immediately, the French-speaking, Sorbonne-trained first lady set about to turn "that dreary Maison Blanche" into a residence to rival Versailles. She conducted research, consulted with experts and previous occupants—including Franklin D. Roosevelt Jr. and President Truman—and decorated the rooms with period art and antiques ranging from Dolley Madison's sofa to George Washington's mirror.

The result, which Jackie showed off in a 1962 televised tour, was a glittering stage for culture, politics, and ceremony on which she and her husband played the starring roles. Such luminaries as composer Leonard Bernstein, poet Robert Frost, Nobel laureates, and foreign dignitaries were counted among the costars, and the program—whether performed by the Vienna Boys Choir, an opera diva, or Pablo Casals (*right*)—was always fit for a king's court.

Famed Spanish cellist Pablo Casals acknowledges the applause of President Ken-or in the East Room of the White House in 1961. The last time the 85-year-old

Robert Frost chats with the president and Jackie in 1962. The poet recited a poem during Kennedy's inauguration ceremony.

"I think this is the most extraordinary collection of talent, of human knowledge . . . ever gathered at the White House, with the possible exception of when Thomas Jefferson dined alone."

John F. Kennedy at a White House dinner honoring 49 Nobel laureates, April 29, 1962

Storybook Children

Despite the public's seemingly insatiable hunger for news about the youngest members of the first family, the Kennedys—and especially Jackie—took pains to make life as normal as possible for Caroline and John Jr. "If you bungle raising your children," Jackie remarked, "I don't think whatever else you do well matters very much."

Sister and brother had the run of the White House, as did their three dogs. They watched state ceremonies on the South Lawn from the Truman Balcony, made themselves at home in the president's work areas *(right)*, and played for hours on a slide and swings Jackie had installed on the lawn outside the Oval Office.

As in any household with children, the parents never knew what to expect. Caroline, for example, once asked the Speaker of the House of Representatives, Sam Rayburn, why he had no hair. And she delighted all when she tottered into a press conference in Jackie's high heels and, on another occasion, informed reporters that her father was "sitting upstairs with his shoes and socks off, not doing anything."

A giggly pair of Kennedy hobgoblins—a two-year-old clown and a five-year-old witch toting a black kitten—drop by the Oval Office on October 31, 1963, to trick-or-treat with their late-working father.

Two weeks after learning to walk, John Jr. plays cave while Dad looks over papers in the Oval Office. The youngster peeks from a doorway in the photo opposite, snapped as Caroline ducked through the president's legs in spring 1963.

Hail Queen Jackie

Jackie casts an expert eye at Sardar, the horse Pakistani president Mohammed Ayub Khan brought with him on a 1962 visit to the United States. He so admired the first lady's horsewomanship that he later gave Sardar to her.

Weighty matters of state motivated the new president to travel to Canada, France, and Austria in spring 1961, yet everywhere he went it was his wife who stole the show. In Ottawa she was praised for her "charm, beauty, vivacity, and grace of mind." In Paris the papers called her *charmante*. Cameras flashed and huge crowds cried "Jacqui!" whenever she appeared.

By the end of the trip, the first lady had charmed two of the world's crustiest leaders, France's Charles de Gaulle and Russia's Nikita Khrushchev. Asked to pose shaking hands with the president, the Soviet premier looked admiringly at Jackie and replied, "I'd like to shake her hand first."

And she was even more popular back home. Women adopted her bouffant hairdo, pillbox hat, and preference for pink. Jackie look-alike contests abounded, along with copies of her clothes. And hardly a newspaper went to press without word on her comings and goings, her children, or her beloved horses.

"Not since Dolley Madison," Time wrote of Jackie, seen here during her husband's presidential campaign, had a first lady "dressed as elegantly, entertained as imaginatively, or so clearly seen both functions as a creative contribution to the success of an Administration."

The first lady draws an approving glance at a White House reception in September 1961. "Jackie's taste was very simple," said Oleg Cassini, who designed her black and gold gown. "She liked only the very best."

Wearing a red wool suit inspired by the uniforms of the Royal Canadian Mounted Police, Jackie inspects the Mounties' horses during a May 1961 state visit to Canada. Her clothes attracted as much attention as her husband's agenda.

Lord and Master

John Kennedy had a well-earned reputation as a playboy when friends introduced him to Jackie Bouvier in 1952. Wealthy, handsome, and articulate, he was, as the *Saturday Evening Post* put it, "the Senate's gay young bachelor." Biographer William Manchester observed, "When he entered a room with his curious gait, half lope and half glide, women perked up and patted their hair." Kennedy seldom got the cold shoulder, even when he was a teenager. According to his prep-school roommate Lem Billings, "Jack always had lots of girls and did quite well with them."

From Kennedy's earliest days as a novice campaigner—he first ran for office in 1946, winning a seat in Congress—his charisma drew women to him in droves. One Democratic senator described Kennedy's ardent female followers as "jumpers, shriekers, huggers, and touchers." Out on the campaign trail, they gazed at him with all the emotion of love-struck Elvis Presley fans and closed their eyes in bliss when they got close enough to grab his hand and shake it. Kennedy enjoyed the adulation and used it to his political advantage.

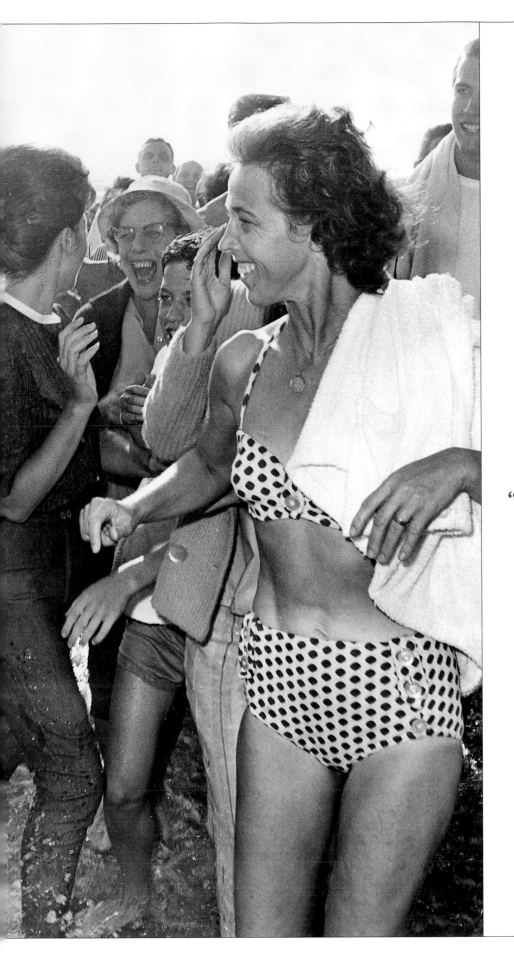

After he became engaged to Jackie, he joked in a letter to a friend that his marriage meant "the end of a promising political career as it has been based up to now almost completely on the old sex appeal."

The pair were wed in 1953, but by 1960 rumors were circulating about the president's wandering eye and unhappy marriage. But Kennedy loved his children deeply, and when his third child, Patrick, died two days after birth in August 1963, he sought solace in Jackie's arms. As they traveled together to Dallas in November, they were said to be as close as they had ever been.

"Am getting married this fall. This means the end of a promising political career as it has been based up to now almost completely on the old sex appeal."

John F. Kennedy in a letter, 1953

Thrilled to be in the right place at the right time, beachgoers in Santa Monica, California, flock around the president during a swing he made through the West in 1962. The first lady was vacationing in Italy.

> "The people who are the best off are the people whose advice is not taken, because whatever we do is filled with hazards."
>
> John F. Kennedy, during the Cuban missile crisis, October 22, 1962

Candidate Kennedy consults with his campaign manager and future attorney general Robert Kennedy during the 1960 Democratic convention. Called "the brother within" by John, the younger Kennedy was the president's closest confidant throughout his administration.

The Burdens of the Office

"When I ran for the presidency of the United States," John Kennedy said on July 25, 1961, "I knew that this country faced serious challenges, but I could not realize, nor could any man realize who does not bear the burden of this office, how heavy and constant would be those burdens."

In the first six months of his administration, he had ordered a disastrous invasion of Cuba at the Bay of Pigs and sent federal marshals to protect civil rights protesters traveling from Washington to New Orleans *(page 66)*. Now, in a nationally televised address, he described the latest emergency—an attempt by Soviet leader Nikita Khrushchev to bully the Allies out of Berlin.

The crisis, which ended with a wall that divided the city for almost 30 years, was the tensest moment of the Cold War to date. But a more harrowing drama awaited—the Cuban missile crisis.

It began on October 14, 1962, when an American spy plane detected launch sites for Russian offensive missiles in Cuba. After eight days of intense private debate with his younger brother and attorney general Bobby *(left)* and the other members of his Executive Committee, or ExComm, the president publicly announced a naval blockade. Then, as the frightened nation faced the very real possibility of nuclear war, he secretly signaled his willingness to dismantle American missiles in Turkey if the Soviets removed their weapons from Cuba. Khrushchev agreed to the swap the following day.

As if chastened by the crisis, Kennedy and Khrushchev later signed a groundbreaking treaty barring atmospheric, underwater, and space testing of nuclear weapons. The pact would be considered Kennedy's greatest achievement.

Kennedy winces as U.N. ambassador Adlai Stevenson reports on Congo premier Patrice Lumumba's assassination in January 1961. At the time the United States and the Soviet Union were vying for influence in the African nation.

A Tragic End

Almost everyone alive at the time remembers where she or he was when the news broke on Friday, November 22, 1963: The president had been slain in Dallas. Police had arrested a suspect, Lee Harvey Oswald, and Lyndon Johnson—sworn in aboard Air Force One as Mrs. Kennedy stood at his side—was the new president.

On Sunday 250,000 mourners filed past Kennedy's body as it lay in state in the Capitol. And just as many lined the route taken the next day by the somber procession that bore the casket to Saint Matthew's Cathedral and on to Arlington National Cemetery, where he was buried.

America looked for a thread of reason in the tragedy but found nothing. Said newscaster David Brinkley, "It was too big, too sudden, too overwhelming, and it meant too much."

It was Jackie who described best what was lost. Recalling how her husband loved the musical *Camelot,* she likened his administration to the reign of King Arthur. "Don't let it be forgot," she said, reciting lines from *Camelot's* title song, "that once there was a spot, for one brief shining moment that was known as Camelot."

The president and the first lady happily greet well-wishers at Love Field before their 20-car motorcade starts the seven-mile drive to Dallas on November 22.

Jackie moves to her husband's aid moments after the first of two bullets strikes him. Abraham Zapruder, a home-movie buff, recorded the scene as the president's motorcade, nearing the end of its route, passed him at Dealey Plaza.

Jackie (right) grieves beside her husband's grave on November 25, 1963, the day he was laid to rest. She holds the flag that covered the president's coffin during the procession from Saint Matthew's Cathedral to the cemetery.

At War
With Jim Crow

★

THE FIGHT FOR EQUAL RIGHTS

To be a Negro in this country and to be relatively conscious," wrote author-activist James Baldwin in 1961, "is to be in a rage all the time." Harsh sentiments, yet ones that found powerful echoes among many black Americans. The '50s had seen undeniable progress in the struggle for racial equality: In 1954, the Supreme Court struck down segregation in the nation's public schools; two years later, a boycott desegregated the buses in Montgomery, Alabama. Moreover, a charismatic leader had come forward who inspired hope and resolution—the Reverend Martin Luther King Jr.

Still, as 1960 began, Jim Crow remained the law of the land. In the Deep South, a black person could not drink from the same water fountain, use the same rest room, or swear on the same Bible as his white brethren. And, despite the Supreme Court's 1954 ruling, the South had adopted a policy of massive resistance to school desegregation. It was time for action.

On February 1, four black college freshmen entered a Woolworth's five-and-dime in Greensboro, North Carolina. Neatly dressed and polite, the young men seated themselves at the whites-only lunch counter and ordered coffee. They were refused. It was 4:30 p.m.; they sat quietly until the store closed at 5:30.

The students returned the next day with 20 companions. The third day there were

Whites attack a black student at a Nashville lunch counter in 1960. "These students are not struggling for themselves alone," said Martin Luther King. "They are seeking to save the soul of America."

A bus-station sign in the South designates the waiting room for blacks. In Florida, racism dictated different textbooks for blacks and whites.

A poor Alabama woman and her children stand beside their weather-beaten house. One-third of blacks lived in poverty in the '60s.

more than 60. Their actions made news, and the news encouraged other students, some of them sympathetic whites. Within two months, the sit-ins had spread to 54 cities in nine states.

Whites reacted in fury, dousing protesters with ammonia, yanking them from their seats, pummeling them, and jailing them for disorderly conduct. When black leaders raised bail, the students opted for jail instead. Other blacks organized boycotts and marched in protest—to be met by police billy clubs and savage dogs.

The blacks did not in any way retaliate, for despite their anger, a cardinal tenet of the civil rights movement was nonviolence. King and other leaders took their lessons from Mohandas Gandhi and counseled pacifism in every encounter. The young people themselves established a Student Non-Violent Coordinating Committee (SNCC) so effective that King could say in April, "Segregation is on its deathbed now, and the only uncertain thing about it is when it will be buried."

The interment had already begun the month before, when San Antonio, Texas, became the first large southern city to integrate its lunch counters. In Nashville in April, the dynamiting of a black councilman's home so appalled the white mayor that he turned his back on segregationists—after which the city's merchants started opening their counters. The struggle in Greensboro was won by July, and by year's end other southern towns had bowed to student demands for equality.

Meanwhile, a parallel movement was forming. In December 1960, the Supreme Court declared segregation illegal in interstate bus terminals. Yet the Kennedy administration, installed in January 1961, showed little enthusiasm for enforcing the ruling. So James Farmer, national director of the Congress of Racial Equality (CORE), made plans to send interracial groups of "Freedom Riders" on bus trips through the South. At every stop, blacks would attempt to use the whites-only facilities, knowing that they would face serious consequences. Said Farmer, "We felt that we could count on the racists of the South to create a crisis so that the federal government would be compelled to enforce the law."

The Grand Dragon of North Carolina's Ku Klux Klan (right) and two Klan members attend a rally. Many local police officers had cordial relations with the KKK and ignored or even conspired in Klan assaults on blacks.

The first Freedom Riders, seven blacks and six whites, left Washington, D.C., for New Orleans on May 4, 1961. Reaching Atlanta on May 14, they split into two groups, one heading for Birmingham, Alabama, the other stopping 60 miles east at the town of Anniston.

The racists were waiting. In Anniston, a mob smashed the bus's windows and slashed its tires, then raced in pursuit when the driver hit the gas. The tires went flat six miles out of town, and someone threw a firebomb into the immobilized bus. The Freedom Riders barely escaped with their lives as the crowd shouted, "Let's roast the niggers!" Next day, photos of the burning bus were on front pages of newspapers across the country *(right)*.

Birmingham was worse. At the bus terminal Klansmen battered the Freedom Riders with baseball bats, lead pipes, and bicycle chains. The assault went on for 15 minutes before police arrived. Public Safety Commissioner Eugene "Bull" Connor blandly explained that since it was Mother's Day most of his men were visiting their mothers. One of the Riders required 53 stitches to close his head wounds; another suffered permanent brain damage.

A week later, racists in Montgomery, Alabama, attacked 21 more Freedom Riders with such ferocity that Washington finally sent in 650 U.S. marshals. On May 21 the lawmen used tear gas to protect a church where Martin Luther King was rallying 1,500 people. "Fear not," said King, amid the acrid fumes and crash of breaking bottles. "We've come too far to turn back." The campaign then shifted to Mississippi, where Freedom Riders arrived by the hundreds all summer long, only to be arrested on such charges as trespassing and breaching the peace. The Riders turned down bail and refused to pay fines. That suited CORE's Farmer. "Fill up the jails, as Gandhi did in India," he said. "Fill them to bursting if we have to."

At last, on September 22, the Kennedy administration petitioned the Interstate Commerce Commission to forbid common carriers to use segregated terminals. In this one area, racial injustice would soon be just a memory. Yet much more remained to overcome.

Freedom Riders and other passengers survey their firebombed bus outside Anniston, Alabama, in May 1961. "When you go somewhere looking for trouble, you usually find it" was the reaction of Alabama's governor John Patterson.

"We will win our freedom because the sacred heritage of our nation and the eternal will of God are embodied in our echoing demands."

Martin Luther King Jr., "Letter From a Birmingham Jail," April 1963

Dr. King ponders tactics from solitary confinement in Birmingham following his 13th arrest since becoming a civil rights leader. Jailers did not let him have a mattress for his cot, forcing him to sleep on the metal slats.

Children's Crusade in Birmingham

Martin Luther King and his colleagues called it Project C—for Confrontation. Its target was Birmingham, a town known to blacks as the "worst big city in the U.S.A.," where virtually everything was segregated. The campaign to desegregate the city at least partially began on April 3, 1963, with sit-ins. Commissioner of Public Safety Bull Connor's force retaliated by arresting 150 protesters, including King. Thrown into solitary confinement, he penned a reply to clergymen who accused him of demanding too much too soon. "For years now," he wrote, "I have heard the word 'wait.' . . . This 'wait' has almost always meant 'never.' "

Out on bail after eight days, the leader initiated a "Children's Crusade" of protest marchers. Some people were aghast. But King's compatriot Ralph Abernathy explained why children were willing to join the demonstrations: "Don't think the smallest ones don't know what they want. They do. They know they can't go to Kiddieland and ride the ponies like the white kids." The children, some as young as six, began their demonstrations on the second of May; 959 were jailed. The next day, Connor's men shocked television viewers across the nation by going after the youngsters with night sticks, attack dogs *(right)*, and fire hoses powerful enough to rip the bark off trees *(pages 8-9)*.

As the marches continued, the city's merchants, already suffering from the disturbances, decided to negotiate. On May 10, King and his allies announced that the businesses had met their demands for desegregation of lunch counters and other facilities and for job opportunities for blacks. Birmingham had reached an accord with its conscience. And thanks to television, the demonstrations had forced Americans all over the nation to recognize the ugliness of racial discrimination.

A Birmingham cop grabs a black man while a dog, jaws open, lunges at him. Commissioner of Public Safety Bull Connor instructed his men to let white onlookers move closer. "I want 'em to see the dogs work," he said. "Look at those niggers run."

"I have a dream that one day . . . sons of former slaves and the sons of former slave owners will be able to sit down together at the table of brotherhood."

Martin Luther King Jr.,
Washington, D.C., 1963

In the largest such demonstration to date in the nation's capital, a quarter of a million people rally in support of civil rights.

The March on Washington

At age 74, A. Philip Randolph had been championing civil rights since before many of the younger leaders were born. The founder and president of the Brotherhood of Sleeping Car Porters, he and his union were dubbed "civil rights missionaries on wheels." In 1941, they announced plans for a march on wartime Washington to demand more jobs for blacks in defense plants. Franklin Roosevelt responded by issuing an executive order banning employment discrimination in government and defense industries.

Now, in 1963, Randolph mapped another march—again for jobs, but also in support of public-school integration and the passage of a fair-employment-practices bill and an omnibus civil rights act. Moreover, a march would unify the movement and turn the national spotlight on key black leaders including Randolph, his aide Bayard Rustin, the Southern Christian Leadership Conference's Martin Luther King Jr., CORE's James Farmer, the NAACP's executive director Roy Wilkins, and John Lewis, chairman of SNCC.

The organizers hoped for 100,000 people. They got 250,000, including thousands of whites. On August 28, the marchers stood at the Lincoln Memorial, where Randolph told them, "Let the nation and the world know the meaning of our numbers. . . . We are the advance guard of a massive moral revolution for jobs and freedom." When King's turn came, he spoke in a voice filled with love and determination. Despite all the injustices, he said, he still had a dream. It was a dream rooted in the American credo that all men are created equal, a dream that black and white youngsters would one day join hands as sisters and brothers. Then, said King, they would sing, "Free at last! Free at last! Thank God Almighty, we are free at last!"

King speaks to the Washington marchers on August 28, 1963 (right). His oratory, said colleague Ralph Abernathy, "was a prophecy of pure hope at a time when black people and the nation as a whole needed hope more than anything else."

Freedom Summer in Mississippi

etween 1962 and 1964, intense effort produced voter-registration breakthroughs for southern blacks in state after state. But not in diehard Mississippi, where only 3,871 new names had been added to the 27,791 already on the rolls, leaving 400,000 adult blacks still ineligible to vote.

To change these abysmal numbers, in 1964 civil rights groups launched an ambitious voting rights project known as Freedom Summer. Central to the plan was a massive registration drive mounted by volunteers, many of them white college students from northern schools. Of equal importance was a new political body, the Mississippi Freedom Democratic Party (MFDP), which was formed to challenge the state's Jim Crow organization at the Democratic National Convention in August.

Mississippi's racists reacted as to a declaration of war. At an orientation session in Ohio, James Foreman warned volunteers, "I may be killed. You may be killed." That chilling possibility became a

Locking hands and singing, the first contingent of Freedom Summer volunteers prepare to leave their Ohio training center for Mississippi.

reality on June 21, when three young workers—James Chaney, 21, a black Mississippian, along with Andrew Goodman, 21, and Michael Schwerner, 24, both white *(right)*—were murdered by Klansmen in rural Neshoba County. Twenty-one men, including county sheriff Lawrence Rainey and a deputy, were later accused of the crime but never went to trial. If the idea was to scare the volunteers away, it failed. All summer long they prepared blacks for registration and recruited members for the MFDP, which grew to 80,000.

That August at the Democratic convention in Atlantic City, the MFDP challenged the all-white regular party delegation, putting forward an alternate delegation composed of 64 blacks and four whites. Anxious to avoid controversy, President Johnson tried to appease the MFDP delegates by offering them two voting seats. They rejected the president's offer, but they did secure one major victory: a pledge that the Democratic Party would never again seat a segregated delegation.

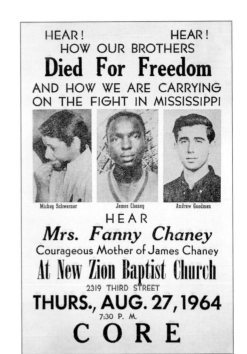

Looking nonchalant, Sheriff Lawrence Rainey (right) and a deputy, Cecil Price, are arraigned in the 1964 murders of three civil rights workers.

The Selma Movement

In early 1965, Martin Luther King targeted Dallas County, Alabama, as the place to push for a strong federal voting rights law; of the county's 15,115 voting-age blacks, only 320 were registered. King counted on the violent reaction of his enemies to dramatize the need for such a law, and they played directly into his hands.

On January 25, while breaking up a peaceful protest march, the county sheriff battered a black woman with his night stick while three deputies pinioned her arms. On February 10, the sheriff's men brutalized student demonstrators with electric cattle prods. On March 7, Alabama troopers clubbed and tear-gassed 525 blacks marching from the county seat, Selma, to Montgomery, the state capital *(right)*. On March 9, four goons murdered a white minister from Boston who had come to Selma to take part in the protests.

With waves of revulsion sweeping the country, President Johnson went before Congress with a voting rights bill and sent troops to protect the marchers. The marchers resumed their trek on March 21, reaching the capital four days later. The Voting Rights Bill became law on August 6.

Protected by federal troops and with Martin Luther King leading the way, marchers head

His agenda emblazoned on his forehead, a young activist pauses en route to Montgomery, where the marchers from Selma were joined by 25,000 supporters.

down Highway 80 from Selma to Montgomery.

Sheriff's deputies and demonstrators confront one another. Among the protesters in the Selma movement were 450 religious leaders from all over the country.

The Debacle in Memphis

It was one of those mean, stupid little acts guaranteed to outrage black people. One rainy February day in 1968, the city of Memphis sent its black garbagemen home early and paid them for only two hours, while white workers received a full day's pay. The 1,300 recently unionized blacks went out on strike, and the next weeks saw an escalating conflict, with the mayor refusing to negotiate and threatening to fire the strikers.

At the urging of black leaders, Martin Luther King came to Memphis to help break the stalemate. Speaking on March 18 to 17,000 people at the city's Mason Temple, he called for a massive nonviolent march to demonstrate their resolve to win equity for black workers. "Try it," he cried, "and they will hear you." He himself would return to the city in 10 days to lead the protest.

But King was unaware that some angry Memphis youths had rejected nonviolence and were talking about riots and quoting Black Power advocate H. Rap Brown that blacks "must move from resistance to aggression, from revolt to revolution."

The march on March 28 was a debacle. No sooner had it begun than teenagers started smashing windows and looting stores. King acted instantly. "I will never lead a violent march, so please call it off," the Nobel Peace laureate told a colleague. But peace had no place in Memphis that day. Police charged the marchers, gassing, clubbing, and eventually shooting; a black youth was slain and 60 people injured.

At his motel King listened, horrified, to his aides' reports on the violence. For long minutes he despaired. Then he said, "We must come back. Nonviolence as a concept is now on trial."

With placards proclaiming their faith in themselves and their cause, striking Memphis sanitation workers prepare for their protest on March 28, 1968.

"I May Not Get There With You"

Coretta Scott King (opposite) comforts her daughter Bernice at her husband's funeral in Atlanta. The man who had fought so valiantly for the poor was borne to his final resting place in a farm cart drawn by two mules.

As King lies dying, aides point to the direction of the rifle shot. An escaped convict named James Earl Ray was sentenced to life in prison for the assassination in 1969.

A deeply depressed Martin Luther King returned to Memphis on April 3 amid charges in the press that he was a wolf in pastor's clothing, "talking nonviolence even as it erupts all about him." Nevertheless, he and his aides set to work planning a second march, calling on labor leaders, churchmen, and entertainers to join them.

His spirits lifted in the course of addressing 2,000 supporters at Mason Temple that evening. He told them that he saw God's will at work, that men were rising up in South Africa, in New York City, in Atlanta, in Memphis, always with the same cry: "We want to be free." God, said King, "has allowed me to go up to the mountain. And I've seen the Promised Land. And I may not get there with you. But I want you to know tonight that we as a people *will* get to the Promised Land."

The next day was filled with planning, and King looked forward to dinner with friends that evening. He was standing on his motel balcony about to depart when a rifle shot rang out. The .30-06 slug tore off part of his jaw, fractured his spine, and severed vital arteries. Doctors at St. Joseph's Hospital declared the great man dead at 7:05 p.m.

Big Screen, Little Screen

★

Struggling to lure audiences away from their television sets, movies in the '60s got bigger, more expensive to make (and to see), more spectacular, and more venturesome. They took on more mature themes. They got sexier and bloodier. And they sparked so much controversy that the film industry in 1968 was forced to replace the Production Code, its means of self-regulation since the 1930s, with a censor-appeasing ratings system of Gs, PGs, Rs, and Xs. Television, by contrast, remained mostly tame, timid, and tepid— "a vast wasteland," Federal Communications Commission chairman Newton Minow famously called it at the start of the decade. It was true that the networks served up huge helpings of pablum, but some of the shows that debuted in the '60s had a welcome bite to them.

The syrupy suburban family sitcoms of the '50s, for instance, underwent strange inversions. In *The Flintstones (inset)*, the suburbanites moved from the real world to the world of animation and from modernity to the Stone Age. Fred worked a dinosaur bulldozer, yelled "Yabba-dabba-doo!" at quittin' time, and raced home to Wilma in a car he powered with his feet. In *The Addams Family*, Gomez, Morticia, and their creature-feature kin *(page 83)* raised carnivorous plants, fished with dynamite, and stretched one another on a rack in the basement, but within their own eccentric

---

Young Benjamin Braddock (Dustin Hoffman) eyes the silken leg of his middle-aged seducer, Mrs. Robinson (Anne Bancroft), during the pair's loveless and mechanical affair in the 1967 film The Graduate.

Maxwell Smart (Don Adams) talks on his shoe phone. As Agent 86, Smart routinely saved the world, although almost always by accident.

Batman (Adam West) alights to save Gotham City by thwarting a host of oddball evildoers.

parameters they were models of taste and decorum, eerily upper class.

Not so the Clampett clan of *The Beverly Hillbillies (page 85)*, who remained Ozark cornpone even after they struck oil and moved to California's poshest preserve. Millions tuned in weekly to watch down-to-earth Jed Clampett and his fish-out-of-water but very rich tribe get the drop on their snobbish neighbors. Critics sneered at the show, but it bubbled like black gold to the top of the ratings three weeks after its premiere and stayed there for two years.

Maxwell Smart, the main character of the espionage spoof *Get Smart! (left)*, was another lovable innocent. As bumbling Agent 86 for a supersecret spy agency, Don Adams had just as many gismos as James Bond, but somehow he never got quite the same results. He made "Sorry about that, Chief!" and "Would you believe . . . ?" staples of popular speech.

Camp came to television in 1966 in the person of Batman *(below, left)*. Ably assisted by Robin the Boy Wonder, the serious, square-jawed, caped crusader was a caricature of right-thinking comic-book superheroes, lecturing on good citizenship even as he struggled to escape the snares of the Joker, the Penguin, and other engaging villains.

Striving to be not just novel but hip, television in 1968 acknowledged the youth counterculture and its antiheroes with *The Mod Squad (page 84)*. Although the show was standard cop fare, its protagonists were decidedly different: three young petty criminals who turned their lives around after being recruited for police work. Peggy Lipton played a poor runaway and Michael Cole an angst-ridden dropout from the upper middle class. Hippest of all was Clarence Williams III as Linc Hayes, a brooding, philosophically inclined ghetto black.

Linc Hayes was one more step in TV's attempt to introduce some racial reality on the tube. In 1965 it had paired Bill Cosby with white actor Robert Culp in *I Spy (page 85)*, an Emmy-award winner for Cosby. Three years later came *Julia,* starring Diahann Carroll, the first sitcom to focus on a black family.

Uncle Fester (Jackie Coogan) lurks behind Gomez (John Astin), wife Morticia (Carolyn Jones), and children Wednesday (Lisa Loring) and Pugsley (Ken Weatherwax). Grandmama (Blossom Rock) and butler Lurch (Ted Cassidy) complete the Addams household.

Anxious, hunted, at odds with authority, Dr. Richard Kimble of *The Fugitive (right)* was another character who resonated strongly with '60s viewers. On the run from the law after being wrongfully convicted of murdering his wife, Kimble (David Janssen) had to elude his pursuers while searching for the real killer for four prime-time years.

His ordeal lasted one year longer than the prime-time voyage of the USS *Enterprise,* the vehicle for television's first serious venture into outer space, *Star Trek (opposite).* Each week between 1966 and 1969 Captain James T. Kirk and his fictional crew beamed down on strange and wonderful worlds, their phasers set on stun. *Star Trek*'s great appeal, however, lay mainly in inner space, the moral dilemmas confronted by thinking creatures wherever they are.

A "*Wagon Train* to the stars" was how creator Gene Roddenberry envisioned *Star Trek,* touching on an inescapable fact: Whatever its tentative probing of new directions in the '60s, television stayed mainly with the tried and true, including Westerns. The decade began with *Gunsmoke* as the most popular show. *Wagon Train* was the most watched in 1961. And for three seasons, from 1964 to 1966, Adam, Hoss, Little Joe, and Ben Cartwright kept *Bonanza (right)* at the top of the ratings.

The Fugitive, 1963-1967

The Mod Squad, 1968-1973

Bonanza, 1959-1973

Star Trek, 1966-1969

I Spy, 1965-1968

The Beverly Hillbillies,
1962-1971

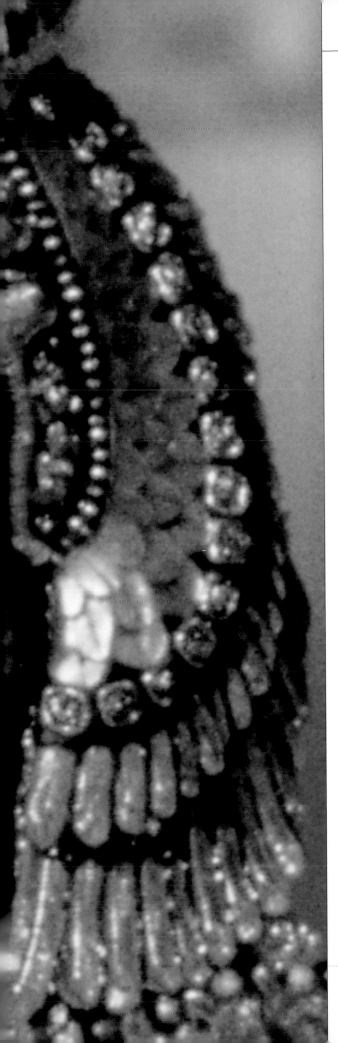

The Queen

For sheer star power, no Hollywood movie queen of the '60s outshone Elizabeth Taylor. Talented, temperamental, prone to wild excess, a veteran of 20 years in show business and four marriages, Taylor had proven herself extraordinary in every way. She was thus a natural for the part of Cleopatra in director Joseph Mankiewicz's 1963 film about the extraordinary Egyptian queen.

Even before its release, *Cleopatra* gained notoriety for being as extravagant as its star. At $40 million it was the most expensive movie ever made; Taylor herself earned an unprecedented $1 million plus overtime. Lavish sets included reconstructions of the Roman Forum and Cleopatra's Alexandrine Palace, both built on location in Rome.

Despite the epic's astronomical cost, audiences were less interested in Taylor's scripted role than in her off-screen seduction of costar Richard Burton, who played Mark Antony. Just as the Roman ruler abandoned his wife for Cleopatra, so Burton left his wife for Taylor. Everyone from Ed Sullivan to the Vatican condemned the pair (Taylor was still married to crooner Eddie Fisher), and Rome's *Il Tempo* fumed that "this vamp who destroys families and shucks husbands like a praying mantis" should be tossed out of Italy as an "undesirable." Studio executives, on the other hand, were upbeat about the affair, hoping that it would generate revenue. "I think the Taylor-Burton association is quite constructive," said producer Darryl Zanuck. A studio publicist was more emphatic: "Everybody, but everybody, will go to see this picture to say that they can see on screen what's going on off it."

Unlike the historical queen of the Nile, who killed herself by placing a poisonous asp at her breast, the undisputed queen of the screen survived. She married Burton in 1964 (only to divorce him, remarry him, and redivorce him later), and together the pair made a series of films, including the 1966 *Who's Afraid of Virginia Woolf?* for which Taylor earned an Oscar as best actress.

In her glittering Egyptian headdress, Queen Liz reigns supreme. Her 65 costume changes for Cleopatra included a gown of 24-karat gold lamé.

Screaming Cinema

Creator of movie thrillers like *The Man Who Knew Too Much, Rear Window, Vertigo,* and *North by Northwest* and since 1955 the host of the often macabre TV show *Alfred Hitchcock Presents,* director Alfred Hitchcock was a master of giving people the creeps. With *Psycho,* released in 1960, he demonstrated that he was also a master of sheer terror.

The movie's female protagonist, Marion Crane (Janet Leigh), has skipped town after stealing $40,000 from her employer and is unlucky enough to find a vacancy at the rundown Bates Motel. Innkeeper Norman Bates (Anthony Perkins) is a charmingly shy homicidal maniac who, dressed as his mother, dispatches Leigh as she showers *(opposite).*

The bloody stabbing—called by one reviewer "one of the scariest pieces of celluloid make-believe ever to run through a projector"—was a new high (or low) in movie violence, and not a few stunned moviegoers went home vowing never to take another shower. *Psycho* opened the door for even bloodier scenes in films to come, including Arthur Penn's *Bonnie and Clyde* (1967). Faye Dunaway and Warren Beatty play Bonnie Parker and Clyde Barrow, an attractive pair of Depression-era backwoods bank robbers who coolly plug their victims as necessary. They get their protracted, slow-motion, gory comeuppance at the film's climax, writhing and withering in a fusillade of lawmen's bullets *(inset).*

Janet Leigh screams in terror during the shower scene in Psycho. Director Alfred Hitchcock took seven days to film the murder, shooting from 70 different camera angles for about 45 seconds of action. A body double stood in for the star, and chocolate sauce, not real blood, gurgled down the drain.

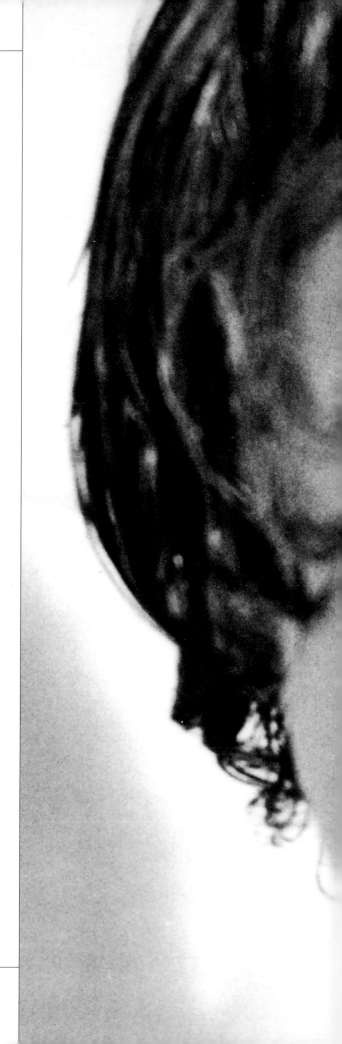

Sexy Stars

Eroticism escalated along with violence in '60s films as an international assortment of beautiful women, some destined to win critical acclaim, began their careers. California-bred Raquel Welch (*right*) made an indelible impact in *One Million Years BC*. Clad in what was billed as "mankind's first bikini," Welch scissored away bits of it for maximum effect. Jane Fonda raised eyebrows and pulses in 1968 as space siren *Barbarella (opposite, left)*. Less adept at English dialogue was voluptuous Swiss beauty Ursula Andress (*opposite, right*), but male moviegoers who saw her as the first Bond girl in 1962's *Dr. No* could not have cared less about her diction. And the all-American good looks of Swedish-born Ann-Margret, marketed as the female answer to Elvis, made her every adolescent boy's fantasy as she wriggled her way through *Bye-Bye Birdie*.

There was nothing sex kittenish about either Catherine Deneuve or Julie Christie. France's exquisite Deneuve rose to stardom in serious films such as Luis Buñuel's *Belle de Jour (opposite, right)*. Britain's Christie was a hauntingly lovely Lara in *Doctor Zhivago* in 1965 (*opposite, right*), the same year she played her Oscar-winning role in *Darling*.

Raquel Welch's best line in One Million Years BC was the cavegirl equivalent of "Giant pterodactyl!" but the body spoke volumes.

Jane Fonda is an alluringly tousled Barbarella. The galaxy-trotting sex goddess was based on a French comic-strip character.

Catherine Deneuve

Julie Christie

Ursula Andress

Ann-Margret

The Name Is Bond, James Bond

"Anyone who has read a thriller by Ian Fleming," wrote *Time* in 1963, "is bloody well aware why the Russians have absquatulated with so many of Britain's state secrets. It's that blinking British Agent 007, it's that blithering bounder James Bond!"

He wore only the finest suits and was fussy about his martinis, which always had to be shaken, not stirred. And he was less interested in hunting Communists, the magazine reported, than ladies. "Agent Bond, in short, is just a great big hairy marshmallow, but he sure does titillate the popular taste."

Sean Connery *(below)* brought the suave and lethal superspy to the screen for the first time in *Dr. No* in 1962, making him the centerpiece of a series that would eventually earn more than $2 billion. Filled with high-tech toys, hairsbreadth escapes, and lots of sex with gorgeous, disposable women, his was the fantasy world of grown-up boys, a fable teetering on the edge of plausibility. "Bond may go wildly beyond the probable," said Fleming, "but not beyond the possible."

The high-water mark for the series was 1964's *Goldfinger,* wherein metal-mad villain Auric Goldfinger sets out to render America's gold supply radioactive and thus untouchable, aided by Oriental factotum Oddball, who wields a deadly blade-brimmed derby. The unflappable Bond survives the hat trick and other assaults and ultimately saves the day. As always.

Bond fails to save one of his lovers (Shirley Eaton), the gilded victim of Goldfinger's Midas touch. Her death leaves the supercool hero shaken but not stirred.

Misfit Heroes

When actor Clint Eastwood wasn't keeping the dogies rollin' as Rowdy Yates on *Rawhide*, a hit for CBS from 1959 to 1966, he was in Italy making the spaghetti Westerns *A Fistful of Dollars* and *For a Few Dollars More*. He completed the trio in 1967 with *The Good, the Bad, and the Ugly*. Eastwood's explosive, taciturn Man With No Name *(inset)* cemented his claim to stardom at a time when anti-Establishment feeling among the young was spawning antihero movies to match, including the 1969 classics *Midnight Cowboy,* starring Jon Voight and Dustin Hoffman, and *Butch Cassidy and the Sundance Kid,* with Paul Newman and Robert Redford.

The cinematic anthem of the genre was *Easy Rider*, produced by Jane Fonda's brother, Peter. He and Dennis Hopper play drug-dealing hippies who ride their Harleys from California to New Orleans to look for America. Joined in mid-odyssey by a disaffected Texas lawyer (Jack Nicholson), the two druggies end up shotgunned by rednecks, but only after taking the ultimate trip— geographically and psychedelically.

Played by Jon Voight, hustler Joe Buck (left) and his grubby pimp Ratso Rizzo (Dustin Hoffman) struggle to survive New York's mean streets in Midnight Cowboy. The x-rated movie won the Oscar for best picture.

The outlaw-heroes played by Paul Newman (left) and Robert Redford try to shoot their way out of a jam at the conclusion of the 1969 film Butch Cassidy and the Sundance Kid, one of the most profitable Westerns of all time.

Dennis Hopper, Peter Fonda, and Jack Nicholson hit the road in Easy Rider. "A man went looking for America," the film's advertising copy says, "and couldn't find it anywhere."

Spaced Out

Critics greeted Stanley Kubrick's *2001: A Space Odyssey* (1968) with cutting reviews. "Lost in the stars," sniffed *The New Republic*. Another critic called it "a sure-fire audience baffler guaranteed to empty any theater of 10 percent of its audience."

But moviegoers spread the word of visual wonders and an enigmatic message. Especially compelling to hip viewers was the dazzling tunnel of light through which astronaut Dave Bowman *(right)* hurtles after he deactivates HAL, his ship's murderous computer. The scene—featuring spectacular, kaleidoscopic color, mountains, a canyon, and a room filled with elegant Louis XVI furniture—was said to be best savored after smoking marijuana.

Debate persisted over the film's meaning. According to one interpretation, Kubrick was saying that humans are clever but infantile creatures whose evolution from apes to tool users to space travelers is guided by something Other, symbolized in the film by black monoliths. The director, however, declined to help people figure it out. "The feel of the experience is the important thing," he said, "not the ability to verbalize it."

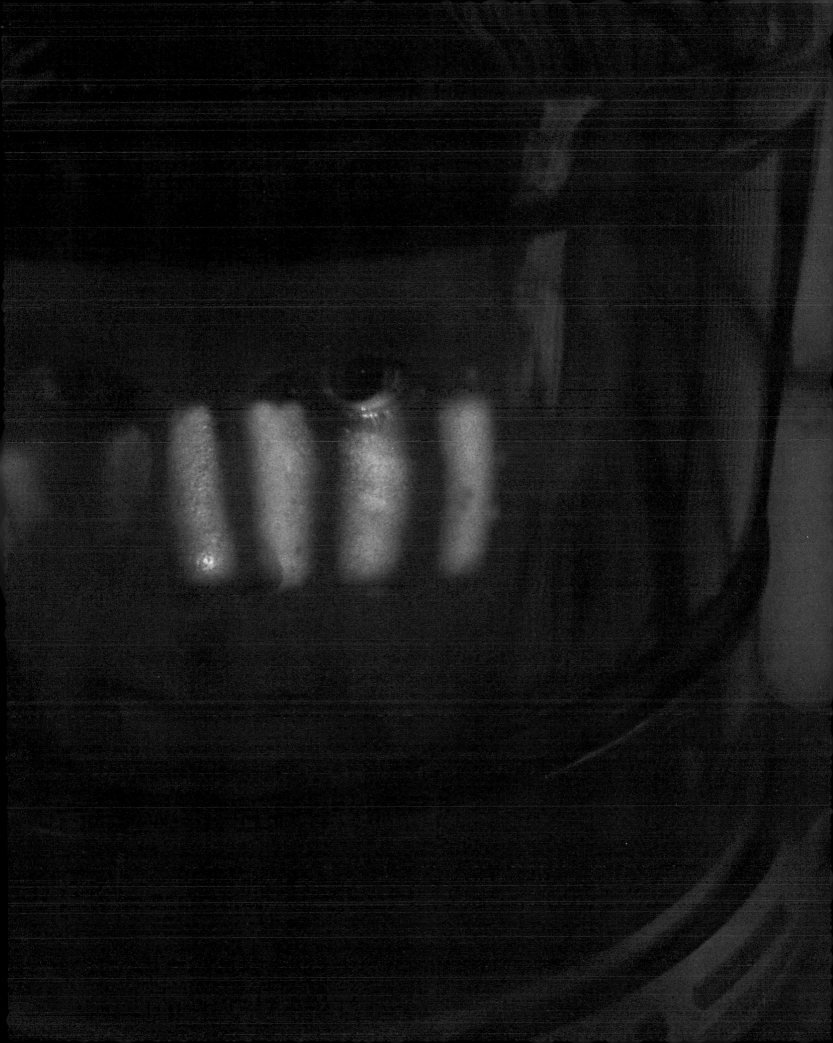

Bigger, Better, and a Lot Richer

★

WHEN SPORT BECAME COMMERCE

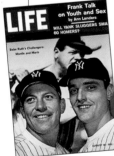

New York Yankees pitcher Whitey Ford once cracked that the ballplayers of the '60s were abandoning the sports pages for the *Wall Street Journal.* Ford was stretching it some, but there was no denying that sports enjoyed a fantastic growth spurt in those years. Pro football went from 12 to 26 franchises and big-league baseball from 16 to 24 clubs with attendance almost doubling, to 27.2 million. But it was television, and not the gate, that powered the surge. For every sunburned bleacherite or blanket-swaddled football nut, many more were cozily ensconced before their tubes.

Eager to capture this ballooning audience, networks willingly paid millions for TV rights, and salaries started skyward as money poured into team coffers. In the 1950s, a pro might make $10,000 a year, but now a college star could rake in a $100,000 bonus just for signing up with a pro team.

As far as fans were concerned, a real hero was worth every nickel. And there were heroes aplenty, like Yankee teammates Mickey Mantle and Roger Maris *(inset, left to right)* vying for Babe Ruth's 34-year-old home-run record, Maris breaking it with a 61st blast on the final day of the season. Here, too, were fresh faces, like Cassius Marcellus Clay Jr., later Muhammad Ali, just 22 and as brash as he was beautiful. "Float like a butterfly, sting like a bee," said Cassius, as he became the most quotable heavyweight champion in history.

Heavyweight champion Muhammad Ali shouts at Sonny Liston after their 1965 rematch. It took Ali only one solid punch in the first minute of round one to down Liston, who had lost the crown to Ali a year earlier.

Football Ascendant

After a dismal afternoon against Cleveland running back Jim Brown, an opponent ruefully remarked, "I made almost as much yardage as he did—riding on his back." Brown epitomized the sort of awesome hero who in the 1960s made football America's number one spectator sport. Meanwhile, TV money and TV exposure made it possible for a smallish city like Green Bay, Wisconsin, to field a club that wowed fans from coast to coast. Led by a genius named Vince Lombardi *(opposite),* the Packers snagged five NFL titles in seven years, plus the first two Super Bowls.

If the Packers were an ode to teamwork, New York Jets quarterback Joe Namath *(inset)* was a study in iconoclasm. "Broadway Joe" loved to party, wore his hair Mod, and had an incandescent lip—as displayed in his cocky comments before the 1969 Super Bowl III. The Baltimore Colts were favored to win, but Namath hooted that the Colts' quarterback was "third string." With thread-needle passing, he broncobusted the Colts by a score of 16 to 7.

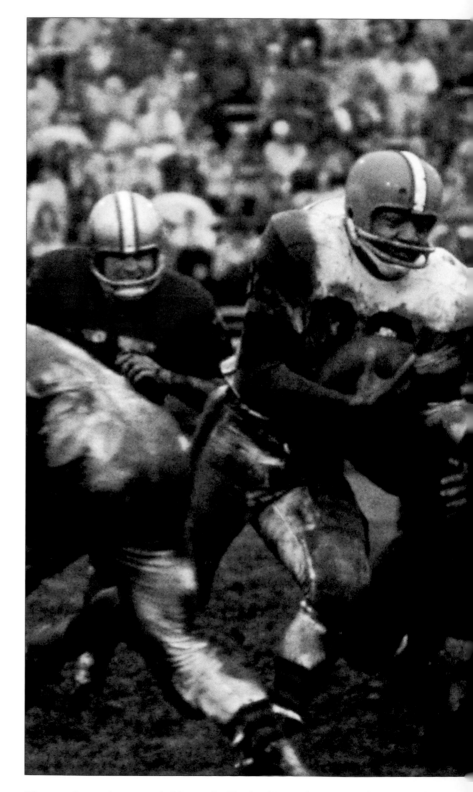

The most devastating runner in history, the Cleveland Browns' Jim Brown drives through

the San Francisco 49ers. Brown's career record of 12,312 yards rushing stood for 20 years.

Lombardi From the Heart

Green Bay Packer guard Jerry Kramer hoists Coach Vince Lombardi aloft after the Super Bowl II victory over the Oakland Raiders.

"It's not whether you get knocked down, it's whether you get up."

"Teams do not go physically flat, but they go mentally stale."

"We are going to win some games. Do you know why? Because you are going to have confidence in me and my system."

"The leader must always walk the tightrope between the consent he must win and the control he must exert."

"If you'll not settle for anything less than your best, you'll be amazed at what you can accomplish in your lives."

"Talent is not only a blessing, it is a burden—as the gifted ones will soon find out."

Baseball Transformed

Change ruled the old ball game in the '60s. It decreed that a half-dozen fine old stadiums like Pittsburgh's Forbes Field must fall to the wrecker's ball. In their place rose bigger, glitzier arenas, some with weather domes and artificial turf to make baseball an indoor sport. The season grew from 154 to 162 games, and more of these were played at night and broadcast on TV to expand the audience.

Traditionalists got a shock when CBS bought the Yankees in 1964. Until then, teams had always been owned by individuals with deep pockets and a passion for the game, and critics said the sale augured a future in which baseball would lose its integrity and become just a way to make a buck.

In another part of New York the Mets, slapstick denizens of the National League cellar, were on their way to a miracle. A roster of rejects thrown together in 1962, the Mets won barely 40 games that year but attracted huge crowds of adoring fans. And so, when 1969 rolled around and the 100-to-1-shot Mets somehow won the World Series, the ticker-tape parade was the greatest the city had seen since V-J Day.

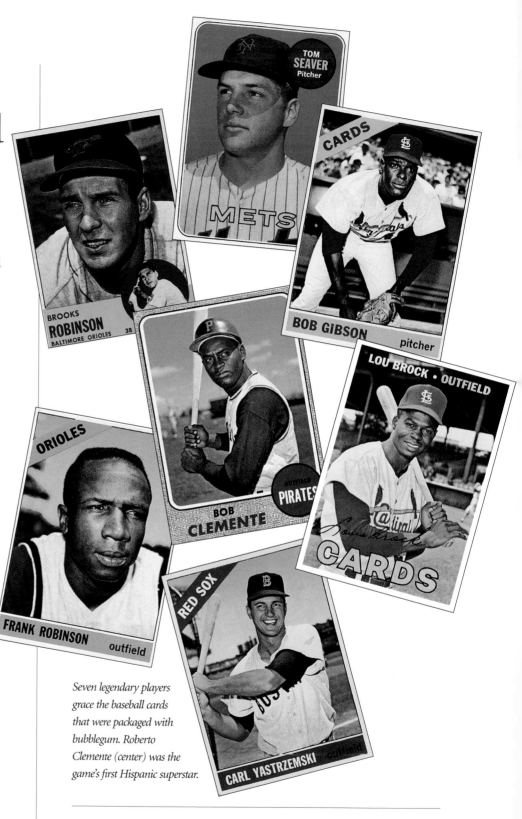

Seven legendary players grace the baseball cards that were packaged with bubblegum. Roberto Clemente (center) was the game's first Hispanic superstar.

Blessed with a blazing fastball, the Los Angeles Dodgers' Sandy Koufax reigned as the game's premier pitcher with 111 wins between 1962 and 1966.

A Decade of Heroes

Of all the fabled teams in American sport, none dominated its game so utterly as basketball's Boston Celtics. Led by playmaker Bob Cousy, rebounder Bill Russell, and forward John Havlicek, the men in green won an astounding nine of 10 championships between 1960 and 1969. "We never got tired of winning," said Cousy. "We'd come back for training camp every year with saliva dripping off our lips, saying 'Kill, kill, kill, I want another title.' "

That ferocious desire to be the best drove competitors all across the spectrum of sports—badminton star Judy Hashman winning 16 national titles, fencer Janice Romary six times triumphant in foils, jockey Bill Hartack collecting the roses in no fewer than four Kentucky Derbies.

The Olympic Games saw the same stupendous performances, with swimmer Don Schollander grabbing four gold medals in 1964 and Al Oerter sweeping the discus in 1960, 1964, and 1968. But the games, so long devoted to the amateur ideal, were under assault by politics and commercialism. With the Cold War raging, athletes now became "national soldiers of sport," and the medal count, U.S. versus U.S.S.R., seemed all-important. Another political current surfaced at the 1968 Mexico City games in the demonstrations by black American athletes impatient for racial progress back home. And merchandisers everywhere exploited the games so blatantly that Olympic boss Avery Brundage complained, "We had Olympic butter, Olympic sugar, Olympic petrol." But commercialism hadn't changed one thing: A champion remained a champion.

How to Destroy a Team

Bill Russell controls the backboard against the Los Angeles Lakers during the 1966 championship. So formidable were the Celtics that they reeled off 20 straight points against the Lakers in one of their title matches. "We were not just beating this team," Russell remembered. "We were destroying it."

Wilma Rudolph's Triple-Header

Long legs driving, U.S. Olympian Wilma Rudolph (left) blazes to a three-yard victory in the 100 meters at the 1960 games in Rome. She also set an Olympic mark for 200 meters and anchored the winning 400-meter relay. The wonder was that she could run at all: She contracted polio in childhood and could not walk unaided for six years.

Bob Beamon's Leap Into Immortality

High-flying long jumper Bob Beamon (right) propels himself toward a landing 29 feet 2½ inches from the takeoff board at the 1968 Olympics in Mexico City. When the 21-year-old was told he had broken the world mark by almost two feet, he sank to his knees and whispered, "Tell me I'm not dreaming."

Bobby Hull's Sizzling Slap Shot

The Chicago Black Hawks' "Golden Jet" rips a record-breaking 51st goal into the net in the 1966 season (below). The most powerful player of his time, Hull could shoot the puck 118.3 miles per hour. Blocking his shot, said a goalie, was "like being slugged with a sledgehammer."

Golf's Great Hail and Farewell

Jack Nicklaus chips to the green while fading giant Arnold Palmer looks on in a composite cover that appeared shortly before the 1965 Masters tournament. Nicklaus shot a record 17 under par, leaving Palmer a distant second and causing golf great and Masters founder Bobby Jones to remark, "Jack is playing a game with which I am not familiar."

Peggy Fleming's 24-Karat Gold

With a solid lead and every reason to play it safe, Peggy Fleming (right) pulls out all the stops in the last part of the figure-skating competition at the 1968 Winter Olympics in Grenoble. "I'm competing against myself," she said. "I'll skate as well as I can." That sort of spirit and artistry won her the only gold medal of the games for an American.

Billie Jean King's Silver Platter

The finest women's tennis player of the decade, Billie Jean King displays her trophy for winning a third straight Wimbledon singles title in 1968. King, whose power-hitting, net-charging game was unprecedented in women's tennis, observed that the sport allowed a woman to "be a champion and a lady at the same time."

A Different Kind of War

★

THE TRAGEDY OF VIETNAM

Americans had never fought a war like it. It was the longest and most unpopular conflict in American history. It was the nation's first and only defeat. And it inflicted wounds so deep that politicians and military leaders would use it for years to come as a model of how not to deploy the nation's military. It was Vietnam.

The United States became involved there in the anxious Red-scare years following the Communist conquest of China in 1949. Vietnam at the time was part of the French colony of Indochina and the home of a dogged Communist uprising led by the charismatic Ho Chi Minh and supported by China and the Soviet Union. Determined to contain the Red menace, President Harry Truman in 1950 sent military aid and a few soldier-advisers to assist the French. Support continued under President Dwight Eisenhower, who in April 1954 described what might befall other Asian nations if the Communists seized power in Indochina: "You have a row of dominoes set up. You knock over the first one, and what will happen to the last one is a certainty that it will go over very quickly. So you could have a beginning of a disintegration that would have the most profound consequences."

A month after Eisenhower's warning, the Communist rebels routed the French. Under

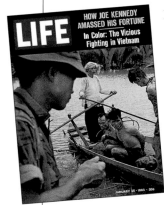

American involvement in Vietnam first made Life's cover in January 1963 (inset). Three years later, more than 300,000 U.S. troops were at war, including the GI at right avoiding enemy fire in a rice paddy.

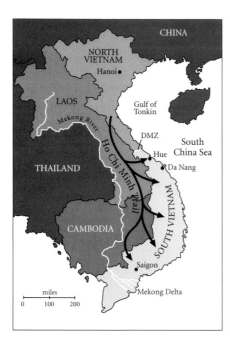

The 1954 Geneva accords divided the former French colony of Indochina into four parts—South Vietnam, North Vietnam, Laos, and Cambodia. The Ho Chi Minh Trail (black arrows), the Vietcong's main supply route, originated in North Vietnam, then passed south and east through Laos and Cambodia before ending south of the demilitarized zone (DMZ) in South Vietnam. The trail was one of the most important targets for American bombers.

Vietnam Service Medal

an international agreement, their former colony was split into Laos, Cambodia, and Vietnam, which was temporarily divided at the 17th parallel into the Communist-held North and the American-backed South. However, South Vietnamese Communists kept up the pressure there.

About 650 Americans a year worked in South Vietnam until 1962, when President John Kennedy upped the number to 12,000. Besides advising, training, and supporting South Vietnam's army, they were increasingly engaged in combat with the Communists, known as the Vietcong or the National Liberation Front.

Despite American efforts to beef up its ally, by 1964 the enemy was in control of much of the South Vietnamese countryside. The Communist success was widely blamed on the South Vietnamese troops, who were ill motivated and poorly led. In the service of graft-ridden military regimes that came and went with revolving-door regularity, the soldiers often fought halfheartedly or not at all; the desertion rate ran as high as one in three.

Lyndon Johnson, now president and commander in chief, privately referred to Vietnam as "a little piss-ant country" and did not think it "worth fighting for," but he feared a devastating political backlash if he tried to reverse U.S. policy there. In August 1964 he seized on exaggerated reports of skirmishes between North Vietnamese torpedo boats and two U.S. destroyers in the Gulf of Tonkin to push a resolution through Congress that dramatically increased his ability to shape events in Vietnam. Passed with only two dissenting votes, the resolution gave the president authority to "take all necessary measures to repel any armed attack against the forces of the United States and to prevent further aggression." A Johnson aide called the measure "the functional equivalent of a declaration of war," while Johnson himself said it was like "grandma's nightshirt" because "you could fit everything under it."

Six months later, the president exercised his new authority following a Vietcong attack on a U.S. base near the provincial capital of Pleiku that left eight Americans dead. He ordered the beginning of Operation Rolling Thunder, a bombing campaign aimed at railroad yards, troop camps, and other targets in North Vietnam. And, in a move that destroyed any illusion that the U.S. role was merely advisory, he dispatched combat troops to South Vietnam. The two battalions of 3,500 marines who came ashore near Da Nang in March were the vanguard of a rapidly escalating American presence that in three years would exceed 540,000 men.

Enemy forces also swelled, with North Vietnamese regulars now invading the South by way of the Ho Chi Minh Trail *(map, opposite)* to reinforce the Vietcong. They encountered the most fearsome concentration of conventional firepower ever unleashed anywhere. In addition to a ground arsenal of automatic weapons, tanks, and artillery and support from ships offshore, the Americans launched an awesome air armada—giant B-52 bombers, sleek F-104 Phantom fighters, and other warplanes capable of raining down a hellish assortment of pellet-filled cluster bombs, the incendiary jellied gasoline known as napalm, chemical defoliants such as Agent Orange, and other modern munitions *(pages 122-123)*. Moreover, the Americans possessed unprecedented combat mobility thanks to the workhorse helicopter. Choppers transported troops into action, served as gunships in support, brought in hot meals and even ice cream, and airlifted the wounded to base hospitals *(pages 124-125)*.

Because the Selective Service System granted deferments to college and graduate-school students for much of the war, the men who employed this high-tech arsenal—nearly three million troops in all— were on average 19 years old, eight years younger than the soldiers who had fought in World War II and Korea. They also came disproportionately from poor, working-class, and minority backgrounds.

The troops saw most of their combat during patrols or in small-unit actions. For these operations, they would be helicptered into a target area where they would fan out in small groups to flush out the enemy. Wading waist deep in flooded rice paddies or cutting through dense jungles, they encountered stifling heat, leeches so tenacious they had to be burned off with cigarettes, and an ingenious array of mines and booby traps. They discovered mortar shells rigged to tripwires, pits bristling with poison-tipped bamboo stakes, even spears lashed to bent saplings and triggered by sudden pressure on a vine or root. At any moment, the shadowy enemy might materialize, darting from the jungle or from hidden tunnels to ambush the Americans.

GIs typically felt they could trust none of the civilians they met.

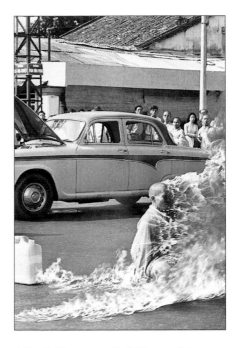

A South Vietnamese Buddhist monk immolates himself to protest the limits imposed on religious freedom for Buddhists by the Catholic-dominated government. The 1963 suicide shocked Americans, who were largely ignorant of Vietnamese affairs.

Shouldering a rocket launcher, a marine fords a waist-deep stream just south of the demilitarized zone in October 1966. He was listed as missing in action 12 days after the picture was taken.

A marine peers from a window in Hue, a city besieged during the Tet offensive in January 1968. Little but rubble remained by February 24, when the city was finally retaken.

South Vietnam's national police chief summarily executes a suspected Vietcong officer in Saigon on February 1, 1968. The scene was seared into the American consciousness by the photograph above and by television footage of the execution.

The Vietcong didn't wear uniforms, so they were nearly impossible to distinguish from noncombatants. "You never knew who was the enemy and who was the friend," recalled a former marine captain, E. J. Banks. "They all dressed alike. They were all Vietnamese. Some of them were Vietcong. . . . The enemy was all around you."

Several times a year massive "search-and-destroy" missions were mounted. In these operations, with code names such as Masher or White Wing, bombers and artillery units would plaster a suspected enemy area. Then a swarm of helicopters jammed with GIs would swoop down, deploying as many as 20,000 troops. The actions incurred heavy casualties on both sides but usually resulted in an American victory and a Communist retreat. Inevitably, however, soon after the GIs had returned to their base camps and American officials had pronounced the area liberated, the guerrillas filtered back in.

The same turf thus had to be fought over again and again. Since there were no front lines and no permanent occupation of territory, the number of enemy dead became the sole measure of progress. "All we did was count," wrote William Broyles, a marine lieutenant. "That was our fundamental military strategy. Body count."

The emphasis on body count and another statistic known as the kill ratio invariably led to inflated numbers. It also provided an incentive for indiscriminate killing. Since GIs rarely could distinguish between civilians and the enemy, both tended to become dehumanized in their eyes, and in the stress of combat anybody could seem fair game. The army massacre of hundreds of old men, women, and children in the hamlet of My Lai in 1968 *(opposite)* shocked but did not surprise veterans of Vietnam.

Early attempts to pacify the South through economic and social reforms—"winning hearts and minds," as the familiar phrase had it—evolved into destruction of the countryside. The total weight of bombs dropped on both North and South Vietnam amounted to four times that used by the United States in all of World War II. So many villages were obliterated that one fourth of the South's population was uprooted. The irony of noble intentions gone awry was nowhere more evident than in the report of an army major after bombs laid to waste the provincial capital of Ben Tre in the Mekong Delta: "We had to destroy the town in order to save it."

Despite such devastation and despite massive enemy casualties—U.S. estimates put the kill ratio at 11 of the enemy to every dead American—the Vietcong and North Vietnamese demonstrated a relentless determination to reunite their nation. To replenish losses, reinforcements and arms poured down the Ho Chi Minh Trail in ever increasing numbers. Even so, in early 1968 American officials were expressing optimism. Half a million troops were in Vietnam, and their commander, General William Westmoreland, professed to see "light at the end of the tunnel." But on January 30, while both sides were observing a truce in honor of Tet, the lunar new year observance, the Communists delivered what *Time* called "an unpleasant, even humiliating surprise": Some 80,000 North Vietnamese and Vietcong troops attacked more than 100 major targets throughout the South, including the U.S. embassy in Saigon and the old imperial capital of Hue, which they held for more than three weeks *(opposite)*.

The offensive failed militarily, but it was the political turning point. In the United States, where opposition to the war had been gathering force for several years *(pages 126-135),* even those who had supported the war were stunned by the enemy's ability to mount a major offensive. "We have been too often disappointed by the optimism of the American leaders, both in Vietnam and in Washington, to have faith any longer in the silver linings they find in darkest clouds," said Walter Cronkite on the CBS Evening News on March 6. "It seems now more certain than ever that the bloody experience in Vietnam is to end in a stalemate." For the first time, more than half of those polled disapproved of Johnson's handling of the war, and he announced he would not run for reelection.

Peace negotiations began in Paris that spring and dragged on for five years. President Richard Nixon started bringing Americans home under his policy of "Vietnamization," but he also widened the war to neighboring Cambodia and Laos. Dispirited GIs increasingly turned to drugs, to the practice of "fragging"—attacking their own officers—and even to desertion. They went home not as heroes but as scapegoats. The last of them left in 1973. Two years later, South Vietnam fell to the Communists, a quarter of a century after the first American was sent to South Vietnam. The futile endeavor to crush Communism there had cost the lives of more than 58,000 Americans.

Unarmed Vietnamese civilians gunned down by American soldiers under the command of U.S. Army Lieutenant William L. Calley Jr. lie on a road leading from the hamlet of My Lai in March 1968.

In 1966, a boy in Massillon, Ohio, watches as marine pallbearers bring home the city's first victim of the war, a 21-year-old private. The grieving father walks behind the casket.

Overleaf: Soldiers confront villagers in a stream near Bong Son, in east-central South Vietnam, in 1966. Sorting out Vietcong from civilians bedeviled GIs throughout the war.

Marines taking part in a search-and-destroy operation hurl hand grenades during close-quarters action on jungle-covered hills near the demilitarized zone in 1968.

"I am writing it in a hurry. I see death coming up the hill."

A GI's last letter home, 1969

During a downpour in June 1967, an American soldier wrapped in his poncho takes a nap atop a sandbagged bunker while a buddy keeps watch. The combatants on both sides had to contend with monsoon rains, boot-deep mud, and devastating heat.

In January 1966, weary GIs (right) rest in a captured enemy trench in a coastal province long dominated by Communists. The soldiers, members of the First Air Cavalry Division, cleared the enemy from the province—but only temporarily.

Fiery tentacles spew from a phosphorus bomb dropped on a village in the central highlands by an American propeller-driven plane in 1966. An armada of more than 3,000 ground- and carrier-based aircraft flew missions in both North and South Vietnam.

Pictures taken by combat photographers helped Americans back home put faces to the weekly casualty reports. Above, a photograph by Larry Burrows that appeared on the cover of Life in April 1965 shows marine James C. Farley, crew chief of a helicopter transporting wounded men back to their base at Da Nang. The soldier in the foreground died moments later. Henri Huet's picture at right made the magazine's cover in 1966. In it, medic Thomas Cole—a bandage covering one eye—tends to a comrade whose wounds were worse than his own. Both Burrows and Huet died covering the war.

The War at Home

★

VIETNAM DIVIDES THE NATION

I n the furious debate over the Vietnam War that polarized the nation, each camp had its own potent symbol. A hand held aloft, fingers forming a V, was a call for peace that was often reinforced by thousands of voices chanting, "Peace now!" Antiwar protesters like those gathered at right in Manhattan in 1969 were denounced as traitorous "peaceniks" by their opponents, who seized on the nation's flag to express support for the war—the only position possible, they said, for a true patriot.

Peace groups began to demonstrate against the war as early as 1963, when the only Americans in Vietnam as yet were military advisers rather than combat troops *(pages 110-125)*, but hardly anyone noticed. As the war escalated, however, so did opposition. Unlike previous wars, this one was brought home by an uncensored flow of vivid photographic and TV images. Horrified by the carnage, college students, political radicals, and a large contingent of mainstream Americans banded together in a movement the likes of which the nation had never seen before. Calling variously for immediate peace negotiations, a bombing halt, or unilateral withdrawal, they paraded, picketed, conducted teach-ins, held candlelight vigils, and staged strikes. A widening chasm separated these so-called doves from the prowar hawks. Some of the hawks held their own prowar protests and clamored for the doves to love their country or leave it. Even so, many hawks eventually turned against the war—not for moral reasons but simply because it seemed unwinnable.

Antiwar poster

Draft-resistance poster

Antiwar poster, 1969

Turmoil on Campus

E ven before the antiwar movement emerged, there were rumblings of unrest on campus. In 1962, the manifesto for a new group called Students for a Democratic Society (SDS) described a college generation "looking uncomfortably to the world we inherit" because of racial bigotry and the Cold War. In 1964, student veterans of the civil rights movement launched the Free Speech

"Hell, no, we won't go!"

Antidraft slogan

Movement at the University of California at Berkeley to protest a campus ban on political activity. Then, soon after the first combat troops were sent to Vietnam in 1965, the nation's first teach-in was held at the University of Michigan, drawing 3,000 teachers and students to discussions about the war. Thereafter, activists at scores of colleges organized teach-ins and began staging protests against both the war and campus policies.

In addition to their opposition to U.S. policy, student protesters were also motivated by dread of the draft. Though college students in good standing were exempt from induction until a lottery was instituted in 1969, burning draft cards became a standard feature at demonstrations. Nearly 100,000 men of draft age—18-and-a-half to 26—fled to Canada or other countries. Many got married, feigned disabilities or homosexuality, or even joined the Reserves or National Guard—gambling correctly that the government would not risk the political cost of calling up units filled with the sons of the upper middle class.

Protest buttons

During protests at Harvard in 1969, the clenched fist on a young man's shirt proclaims his antiwar sentiments. Protesters tore strips from the banner for armbands.

Over 30 but Marching

Although many students professed distrust of anyone over 30, a wide spectrum of older protesters lent credibility to the antiwar movement—clergy, professional people, pacifists, housewives, antinuclear activists, even members of the military.

Benjamin Spock, famed for his book on childcare, was cochair of the Committee for a Sane Nuclear Policy and an old hand at peace protests. In 1968 the genial pediatrician was sentenced to prison for conspiring to counsel draft evaders, a conviction that was later reversed. Martin Luther King Jr., the 1964 Nobel Peace Prize winner, was a relative latecomer to the movement. Reluctant to break with President Johnson because he championed civil rights legislation, King finally came out against the war in 1967.

Older leaders often differed with the aims or tactics of the young, frowning on extremists who demanded immediate withdrawal or marched under the Vietcong flag chanting "Ho, Ho, Ho Chi Minh!" Nevertheless, some of the most radical methods of protest were employed not by fuzzy-cheeked youths but by a pair of Roman Catholic priests (*opposite*).

Benjamin Spock and Martin Luther King Jr. lead a protest march in New York City on April

15, 1967. Sponsored by a broad coalition, the march drew well over 100,000 participants.

The Berrigan Brothers

On May 17, 1968, the two Catholic priests above stood outside Draft Board 33 in Catonsville, Maryland, and calmly broke the law. Father Philip Berrigan (left), 44, and his brother Daniel, 47, were tossing matches into two wire baskets stuffed with records they had stolen from the draft board. Longtime social activists, the Berrigans destroyed the files of 378 men about to be inducted because, they said, they were "Christians who take our faith seriously." Sentenced to prison terms, the Berrigans went underground. Philip was apprehended a few weeks later. Daniel, during his four months of freedom, became the first priest on the FBI's most wanted list. The Berrigans' civil disobedience inspired similar draft-board actions elsewhere.

The Anguish of LBJ's War

Lyndon Johnson made Vietnam *his* war. He personally selected bombing targets. Every morning at 3 o'clock he crawled out of bed to hear the latest reports from Saigon. He agonized over the lengthening list of casualties while trying to ignore the growing legions of demonstrators outside the White House. When liberals who had supported Johnson on civil rights and programs such as Medicare and Head Start broke with him over the war, he denounced them as "nervous Nellies." Critics, he said, only prolonged the war by encouraging the enemy.

The so-called credibility gap between official optimism and harsh reality blew wide open after the Tet offensive in early 1968 *(page 115).* The enemy's ability to mount massive attacks when the United States was supposedly gaining the upper hand turned millions against the war. Senator Eugene McCarthy challenged the president in the New Hampshire Democratic primary and lost by only 230 votes. Then Senator Robert Kennedy joined the fray. On March 31, 1968, realizing at last that he had lost the trust of a divided nation, Johnson announced he would not seek reelection.

On the grounds of the Washington Monument, demonstrators wear black robes and skull

masks on November 27, 1965, to symbolize the U.S. government as the grim reaper.

"Hey, hey, LBJ, how many kids did you kill today?"

Antiwar chant

Four months after announcing he would not seek reelection, President Johnson displays his anguish while listening to a tape in which his marine son-in-law, Chuck Robb, describes his experiences in Vietnam.

133

On Chicago's Michigan Avenue near the site of the Democratic National Convention, protesters try to provoke police with obscene taunts during the turbulent night of August 28, 1968.

"Individual policemen, and lots of them, committed violent acts far in excess of the requisite force for crowd dispersal or arrest."

Report of the Walker commission, 1968

Showdown in Chicago

Although the movement had helped bring down the president, it appeared during the summer of 1968 that his war policies might still prevail. The assassination of Robert Kennedy, who had been leading in the Democratic primaries, virtually assured the nomination of Johnson's own choice, Vice President Hubert Humphrey. Furious at this turn of events, about 10,000 youthful opponents of the war gathered in late August in Chicago, the site of the Democratic National Convention. There were few moderates in the motley group, which included the Yippies, the brash put-on artists of the newly formed Youth International Party who intended to nominate their own candidate, a live pig named Pigasus. Many protesters sought confrontation, and Mayor Richard Daley made sure they got it. He denied permits to demonstrate or camp out in city parks and backed up his hard line with 12,000 police, 5,000 national guardsmen, and 6,000 army regulars.

The two sides skirmished sporadically. Then, on the night of August 28, some 3,000 protesters tried to parade to the convention hall, where delegates were debating party policy on Vietnam. Police blocked the way and then waded into the crowd. They tossed tear gas and flailed about with billy clubs, indiscriminately beating reporters and bystanders as well as protesters. "The whole world is watching," the crowd chanted as television cameras zoomed in. It was also watching the proceedings inside the hall when Senator Abraham Ribicoff of Connecticut denounced the "Gestapo tactics" of the police and Mayor Daley shook his fist at the senator and mouthed obscenities.

The showdown in Chicago shook the movement but did not shatter it. Splinter groups of extremists tested out their belief that it would take violence to end the war. But most activists went on marching peacefully, eventually nudging the new president, Richard Nixon, toward a policy of phased withdrawal from Vietnam.

Police manhandle a protester outside the Hilton Hotel, headquarters for convention delegates. An investigation led by Daniel Walker, president of the Chicago Crime Commission, later concluded that a "police riot" had occurred.

Making Love, Not War

★

THE COUNTERCULTURE

Sometimes I feel like I went to a party in 1963," recalled one Californian, "and it sort of spilled out the door and into the street and covered the world." Fueled by psychedelic drugs, rock music, and heady optimism, a countercultural party swept America in the '60s as hundreds of thousands of young people, many of them from middle- and upper-middle-class homes, began to question Establishment values. They tuned out political and social orthodoxy and turned on to peace, love, and personal freedom.

The hippies, as they were popularly known, were descendants of the Beats, who had blasted the materialism and stifling conformity of the Eisenhower era. While the Beats wore black, this new generation of radicals favored flamboyant colors, feathers, flowers, and beads. To many parents, the counterculture's style was as repugnant as its creed. California's governor Reagan summed up the opposition when he defined a hippie as someone who "dresses like Tarzan, has hair like Jane, and smells like Cheetah."

For the most part, hippies remained disengaged from Establishment controversies. Their politics, if they had any, were gentle and nondoctrinaire. The issue they cared most about was Vietnam. Taking a novel approach to stopping the war, in May 1968 over 600 demonstrators gathered at the Pentagon and attempted to levitate it. Although they failed to get the nation's military headquarters off the ground, they succeeded in leaving their stamp on a generation.

Sharing a blanket, a flower, and a certain careless rapture, a tousled couple let their love shine at Woodstock. "People think love is an emotion," said countercultural hero Ken Kesey. "Love is good sense."

Timothy Leary meditates by candlelight. In 1970 he went to prison in California for drug violations but escaped in less than a month and went underground with the help of the Weathermen, a radical faction of Students for a Democratic Society.

Turning on the World

Legal in the United States until 1966 and cheap to produce, LSD, or lysergic acid diethylamide—popularly known as acid—was the drug of choice for the counterculture's avant-garde. On the East Coast Timothy Leary (who had been fired from Harvard for sharing the drug with his students) established an ashram where followers wore flowing robes, meditated, and sought transcendence in acid. "The aim of all Eastern religion, like the aim of LSD, is basically to get high: that is, to expand your consciousness and find ecstasy and revelation within," he explained. Leary's media-friendly slogans promoting drug use *(right)* became counterculture mantras.

Leary's West Coast counterpart was Ken Kesey, the author of the 1962 novel *One Flew Over the Cuckoo's Nest* and leader of the Merry Pranksters, an entourage of kindred spirits whose aim was to "freak freely." In 1964 a dozen Pranksters embarked on a cross-country tour in a wildly painted bus with a sign warning "Caution: Weird Load." They careened down the highways dropping acid, smoking marijuana *(top right)*, popping pills, reading comic books, and blasting the countryside with their superstereo. Kesey, dressed in a pink kilt, pink socks, and patent-leather shoes, his head swathed in an American flag, perched atop the bus playing the flute —a counterculture Pied Piper chasing his "vision of turning on the world."

> ## "Tune in, turn on, drop out."
>
> Timothy Leary

The Merry Pranksters prepare their 1939 International Harvester school bus for an "Acid Test Graduation." After their cross-country bus tour, the Pranksters staged a series of Acid Tests—huge public parties built around rock music, mind-blowing light shows, free LSD, and a lot of what one marveling reporter called "just plain freaky far-outness."

Seeking Bliss in the Haight

By 1966 San Francisco's shabby Haight-Ashbury district had become the counterculture's epicenter. From across the country rebellious flower children arrived by the thousands seeking a hassle-free place to buy acid, live cheaply, and search for values they couldn't find at home.

The Psychedelic Shop on Haight Street served as the neighborhood's unofficial meeting place and purveyor of such essentials as beads, bells, incense, feathers, books about drugs, and records of both rock and sitar music. The Diggers, an anarchistic street-theater group, dispensed other necessities like clothing, medical care, food, and "surplus energy" at their Free Store. Most of all, the Haight provided a space to just be. Thousands gathered for celebrations like the three-day 1966 Trips Festival *(right),* which featured LSD, the Grateful Dead, strobe lights, and an Olympic trampolinist jumping from a balcony.

Equally blissful was the festival known as the Human Be-In.

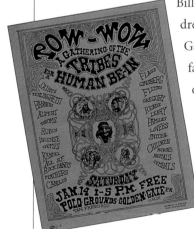

Billed as a "Gathering of the Tribes" *(inset),* it drew 20,000 or so celebrants to nearby Golden Gate Park on January 14, 1967, a date declared favorable by an astrologer. The Diggers passed out acid and turkey sandwiches; Timothy Leary chanted "Tune in, turn on, drop out"; Jefferson Airplane and the Dead played; the Beat poet Allen Ginsberg read poems and purified the ground with Hindu mantras; and everybody was happy, one participant recalled, "simply to be-in—that is, to be in a place declaring your right to be."

In the months that followed, Haight-Ashbury became one gigantic, round-the-clock be-in. It climaxed in 1967's Summer of Love, when 100,000 flower children roamed the Haight in pursuit of bliss.

Communal Life

Filled with the spirit that propelled Americans to head west in earlier times, the pioneers of the counterculture abandoned straight America for communes. In the latter part of the '60s, these new communities attracted people fleeing materialism and conformity. Communes came in great variety, depending on what their members were searching for and hoping to create. At one extreme was the Hog Farm, a self-described "expanded family, mobile hallucination, a sociological experiment, an army of clowns." After living in tents on a hog farm near Los Angeles, the four dozen or so men, women, and children and their pet pig pulled up stakes and became nomads, touring the rock-festival circuit in a fleet of psychedelically painted school buses, vans, and trucks.

The typical commune, though, was a group of like-minded people heading back to the land in search of shared work and spiritual rebirth. Some were united by a particular religion or philosophy. There were Buddhist, Hindu, and Christian communes; polygamous, feminist, and vegetarian ones. Whatever their persuasion, the members bought, rented, or simply squatted on land in the rural reaches of the West, Southwest, and New England. There they built shelters ranging from wigwams and log cabins to geodesic domes, farmed—usually learning as they went, for most commune members had grown up in suburbs and cities—and developed the rituals that made them feel like a family. One group even convinced an ordained minister to marry all its members to one another. "We were standing in a big circle and a cold rain began to fall," a participant recalled of the ceremony. "It was like being married and baptized too."

A few communes thrived. Most, despite the initial enthusiasm of the participants, fell victim to such problems as conflicts over authority, farming failures, or the hostility of neighbors and broke up within a year.

Members of an Oregon commune pose in front of the hexagonal log lodge they built as a meeting place. Their old-fashioned clothes, buckskin, long hair and beards, and Indian ornaments emphasize their pioneering spirit.

"Get it together. . . . Trust. Plant a garden, create a center. Come together."

One commune's credo

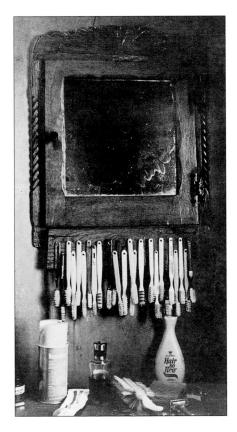

A tidy collection of toothbrushes hangs beneath a bathroom cabinet in a New Mexico commune. Successful communes established orderly routines for chores such as cleaning the house or tending the vegetable garden.

A hippie twosome hawks two newspapers widely read in the Bay Area. The unemployed young were the principal distribution network for alternative publications in California.

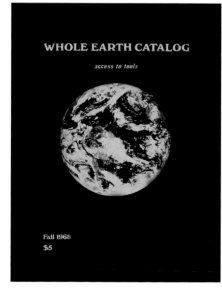

The cover photograph of the first Whole Earth Catalog was taken in 1968 from the Apollo 8 spacecraft. Editor Stewart Brand got the inspiration for the cover during an LSD trip.

The Alternative Press

How can we have a happy, groovy society unless everyone has reached his own nirvana?" asked an editorial in the *Oracle*, a West Coast underground newspaper. Devoted to promoting a groovy society, counterculture publications like the *Oracle*, the Berkeley *Barb*, the Los Angeles *Free Press*, New York's East Village *Other*, and Chicago's *Seed* gave media a new style. The *Oracle*, whose editorial purpose was "to aid people on their trips," offered interviews, poetry, essays on "new science" like astrology and acupuncture, and news about dope. It featured pages of type in vivid rainbow colors, often printed in pictorial shapes rather than in columns. For the *Oracle*, the medium really was the message.

The scene's most enduring publication was *Rolling Stone* magazine, founded in 1967 with $7,500 borrowed by 20-year-old Jann Wenner. The first issue featured a story about the Grateful Dead being busted for drugs at their Haight-Ashbury pad and another article about discrimination against blacks in the television industry. Within two years *Rolling Stone* reached a circulation of more than 64,000 subscribers, swiftly becoming the major chronicler of the rock generation.

For practical instruction about everything from do-it-yourself burials to building geodesic domes, there was entrepreneur Stewart Brand's *Whole Earth Catalog*. Here hippies could purchase a staggering array of products, including tablas (a type of small drum from India), wart removers, macramé cord, organic foods, and Toyota Land Cruisers.

And, for sheer entertainment, there were underground comic books. Graphically sexual and scatological, they held nothing sacred, including their readers. Acid-head cartoonist R. Crumb, for instance, took aim at the "hipper than thou" attitudes of smug counterculturists. Contemplating a world run by hippies, he wrote, "It's frightening!" He envisioned a nightmare of "prison camps full of people not hip enough and prison guards with big peace symbols on their armbands."

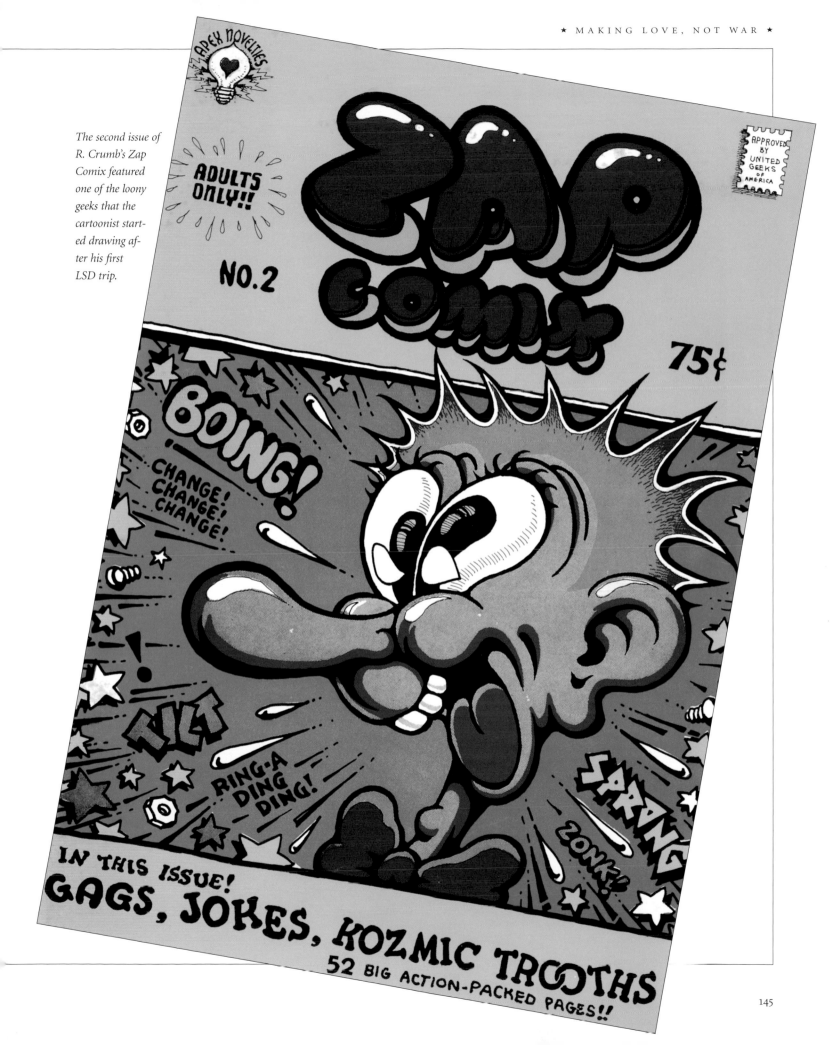

The second issue of R. Crumb's Zap Comix featured one of the loony geeks that the cartoonist started drawing after his first LSD trip.

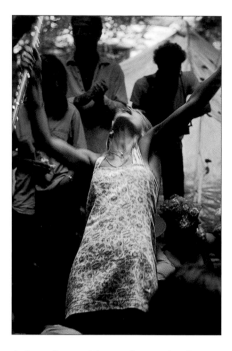

A flute player celebrates the Woodstock spirit, applauded by companions. Shelters (background) were makeshift, but no one cared.

With a pipe to share, a pair of flower children cope with the rain the natural way. Skinny-dipping in farm ponds was popular, too.

Woodstock Nation

There are a hell of a lot of us here," an official announced to the sea of people eddying across Max Yasgur's 600-acre farm on the first day of the Woodstock Music and Art Fair. "If we are going to make it, you had better remember that the guy next to you is your brother."

The man at the microphone had reason to be uneasy. Rock promoters had organized—loosely—a festival for an audience of 50,000 a day, to be held August 15-17, 1969, in the village of Woodstock in upstate New York. When they got wind of the approaching throngs, they rented Yasgur's nearby farm, but they didn't have adequate facilities for the 400,000 people who temporarily turned the festival campgrounds into the third-largest city in New York State. They also hadn't counted on the torrential rains that made the party a mudfest.

It didn't matter. The cheerful crowd ensured that Woodstock was, as advertised, "three days of peace and music." People did remember the guy next to them, and shared food, drugs, tents, sleeping bags, and good humor. Those who ran out of food ate at a free kitchen run by members of the Hog Farm commune *(page 143);* those who had bad trips recovered in a volunteer hospital tent. And wet or dry, everyone danced to the music that blasted almost continuously from speakers mounted on scaffolds. The performers were the best. Richie Havens was there. So were Jefferson Airplane, Janis Joplin, Joan Baez, Santana, Creedence Clearwater Revival, and Sly and the Family Stone.

This was the last, happiest affirmation of the counterculture spirit, which was dissolving in the face of media attention, public hostility, political violence, and an epidemic of hard drugs. Perhaps that's why people would remember Woodstock so fondly. The participants, said comedian Hugh Romney, aka Wavy Gravy, "got the picture of what sharing is about. The music became a soundtrack for that incredible rush of sharing."

Woodstock fans mass by the thousands. "All that energy surging down the hill, focused on one performer," said Joe McDonald of Country Joe and the Fish. "And the roar after a song. It was scary. God, I have never seen so many people."

A Revolution in Music

★

No doubt about it, the '60s rocked. At the start of the decade musicians in Liverpool, in New York's Greenwich Village, in southern California and Detroit and the South were dreaming up sensational new sounds. While the Beach Boys' intricate harmonies celebrated a white suburban utopia, Berry Gordy fused blues and gospel at Motown to create an urban pop sound with soul. The Beatles exploded onto the American scene in early 1964, when young love was still the main concern of pop music. But Bob Dylan was already writing folk lyrics of social and political protest, subjects that would soon begin seeping into rock and roll. Before long, amid the turmoil of the civil rights struggle and the antiwar movement, popular music took on a more experimental, edgier tone.

By 1967 the Beatles' *Sgt. Pepper's Lonely Hearts Club Band* album and LSD-inspired music from San Francisco revealed the impact of psychedelic drugs. Climbing the charts were acid-rock artists such as Janis Joplin, Jefferson Airplane, and guitarist Jimi Hendrix, who in his U.S. debut at the 1967 Monterey Pop Festival stunned the audience by setting his guitar on fire as he played.

Looking back on the immensely creative but tumultuous decade, soul singer James Brown said, "Sometimes I feel like—who's that cat in the Bible with the trouble *and* the faith? Yeeeaaah, now! I'd like to have seen *Job* handle them sixties!"

One of the great virtuosos of '60s rock, Jimi Hendrix (left) sometimes played his Fender Stratocaster with his teeth or behind his back. For blues he preferred the Gibson Flying V, pictured above.

Beach Party

The Beach Boys' endless-summer world of surf and sun evolved from a 16-year-old's brainstorm. Dennis Wilson played in a Los Angeles group that included his brothers Brian and Carl, cousin Mike Love, and neighborhood friend Al Jardine. They were enjoying only modest success, and it occurred to Dennis that they needed a theme—like surfing. He was the group's only surfer, and Brian didn't even like the ocean. Nevertheless, the boys liked the idea, and Brian and Mike collaborated on a happy-go-lucky song called "Surfin'. " It was released on a local label in 1961, and the brothers were riding around in Brian's 1957 Ford when they first heard their record on the radio. That, Dennis recalled, "was the biggest high ever." Carl was so excited he threw up. "Surfin' " was a hit in L.A., and it soon caught on with teenagers who'd never been within a thousand miles of an ocean.

With every new release the Beach Boys loaded their fans into a hot little coupe and sped down the freeway to a Technicolor teen paradise where the surf was always up, there were two leggy girls for every sun-bronzed boy, and everyone's parents were too far away doing dull, adult things to spoil the perpetual beach party. Other California groups *(left)* helped keep the party rocking.

Brian was the artistic genius of the Beach Boys, composing their intricate yet seemingly effortless harmonies and writing the lyrics. Then, in 1966, the group recorded an album with a new sound. Using such instruments as violins and a Japanese zither, Brian's innovative arrangements for *Pet Sounds* drew raves from critics, who declared that the album rivaled the work of the Beatles in creativity.

Instead of the usual sunny fare, *Pet Sounds'* lyrics dwelled on fading love, unfulfilled dreams, fair-weather friends. The album hinted that the party wouldn't go on forever after all. And, in fact, the Beach Boys' popularity faded as the decade wore on. The golden days of good vibrations were over.

From left to right, Beach Boys Brian Wilson, Mike Love, Dennis Wilson, Carl Wilson, and David Marks hold their trademark surfboard. Marks filled in for Beach Boy regular Al Jardine when he left the group for a year and a half.

The Supremes

The Temptations

Mary Wells

Motor Town Music

Motown—the name evokes a wealth of images: the Supremes, resplendent in sequins and bouffant hair; the high-stepping choreography and velvety vocals of the Temptations; Mary Wells, Motown's first female star; the urgent intensity of the Four Tops. These acts and many others were the essence of Motown, and their success grew in large part from the vision, energy, and ambition of one man—Berry Gordy Jr., the founder of Motown Records.

Gordy had been an autoworker before writing a few songs that made the pop charts. In the late 1950s he borrowed money from his family and began producing records. "I worked on the Ford assembly line," Gordy said, "and I thought, 'Why can't we do that with the creative process?'"

Gordy started his own label and signed young black performers he discovered himself. He polished their onstage dress and mannerisms and molded their recordings into an amalgam of gospel, rhythm and blues, and pop. The result was music that was popular across racial lines—what Gordy called "The Sound of Young America."

One of the earliest performers to sign with Gordy was Smokey Robinson. "I showed him about a hundred songs I had written," said Robinson. "He rejected almost everything I had . . . but he set me straight. He became my teacher." Unlike Robinson, most Motown performers didn't write their own songs. Gordy hired songwriters and producers to shape the music—striking gold with the writing trio of Lamont Dozier and brothers Brian and Eddie Holland. During one 3-year period, they amassed 28 Top 20 hits.

Gordy ran such a tight ship that there was even a company song, which had to be sung by participants before every business meeting. By the mid '60s Motown, its roster of artists bolstered by the talents of Marvin Gaye, Gladys Knight and the Pips, and Stevie Wonder, was selling more 45s than any other record company in America.

This poster from a 1967 Detroit show touts some of Motown's best. Gordy often required his artists to tour together to promote the Motown image.

The Four Tops

Folk Rock

Rock and roll got the message in 1965. "Suddenly," *Time* magazine noted, "the shaggy ones are high on a soapbox. Tackling everything from the Peace Corps to the P.T.A., foreign policy to domestic morality, they are sniping away in the name of 'folk rock'—big-beat music with big-message lyrics."

Fusing rock's electric sound with the social and political content of folk music began with Bob Dylan. Part of the Greenwich Village folk scene, he got a boost from diva Joan Baez *(right, with Dylan)* when she introduced him at the 1963 Newport Folk Festival. Dylan burst out of the folk cloister and onto the rock scene with his 1965 album *Bringing It All Back Home.* When he played with a full rock band later that year at Newport, folkie purists booed him roundly, but Dylan shrugged them off. Other musicians followed suit. The Byrds *(inset)* topped the charts with their cover of Dylan's "Mr. Tambourine Man," and P. F. Sloane's antibomb lament "Eve of Destruction" was equally successful. Denounced by some as Communist propaganda, the song was banned by many stations. Said one DJ, "How do you think the enemy will feel with a tune like that No. 1 in America?"

Here Come the Beatles

After the Kennedy assassination in November 1963, Americans were longing for something to make them feel alive again. That something would be the Beatles. "We are the antidote, the medicine man," said Beatles' manager Brian Epstein, "dispensing the balm for a very sick society."

Of course, there were doubters. A top Capitol Records executive proclaimed, "We don't think the Beatles will do anything in this market." But suddenly, in January 1964, seemingly every radio and hi-fi in the land was playing "I Want to Hold Your Hand." Soon the countdown was on to February 9—the date of the Fab Four's U.S. debut on *The Ed Sullivan Show* and the kickoff of Beatlemania, American-style.

Britain was already infected with Beatle fever, of course, and every symptom was contagious. The Liverpool group's sound was fresh, and the lyrics written by John Lennon and Paul McCartney for such tunes as "I Saw Her Standing There" and "She Loves You" were like secrets being shared by a best friend. The Beatles were young and cheeky, and their long hair and quirky good looks were part of their appeal.

Soon teenage American girls were screaming, crying, even passing out at Beatles concerts, while the boys were growing their hair long and sporting high-heeled boots and collarless jackets. When it came to the Beatles, everyone from Elvis, who sent them a telegram of congratulations, to the *Washington Post*, which described them as "asexual and homely," had something to say.

In 1965 the moptops recorded the tracks to *Rubber Soul*, a departure for the band. Moving away from the pure pop sound of their previous work, the group tried out new emotions, such as longing and loss in the lyrics of "In My Life."

Hysterical teenage girls, shrieking their heads off like this audience member at the Beatles' U.S. TV debut on The Ed Sullivan Show, made up the core of the group's fans.

"It is now 6:30 a.m., Beatle-time. They left London 30 minutes ago. They're out over the Atlantic Ocean, headed for New York. The temperature is 32 Beatle degrees."

Disc jockey, WMCA radio, New York City, February 7, 1964

The Beatles land at Kennedy Airport on February 7, 1964, for their first U.S. appearance. George Harrison, who had once visited his sister in America, fretted, "They've got everything over there. What do they want us for?"

Rubber Soul, 1965

Revolver, 1966

Sgt. Pepper's
Lonely Hearts
Club Band, 1967

The "White
Album," 1968

The BEATLES

Abbey Road,
1969

Controversy erupted in 1966 when, during an interview, John said, "We're more popular than Jesus Christ right now." Some American radio stations banned their records, and in South Carolina the Ku Klux Klan nailed their albums to burning crosses and threatened them with harm on their upcoming U.S. tour. John apologized once the group arrived, saying, "I'm sorry I opened my mouth. . . . I couldn't go away knowing that I'd created another little pocket of hate in the world." Even so, the tour was marred by bomb threats and disgruntled fans throwing rotten fruit at the stage.

The boys never toured again. They were sick of touring anyway. "We got worse as musicians," said George, "playing the same old junk every day."

The Beatles' image changed as their interests diverged. John reconnected with an earlier passion—art—and met and began working with Yoko Ono; George studied the sitar and Eastern religions; Paul honed his music; Ringo became a father. Yet they continued recording, in 1967 producing perhaps their seminal work—*Sgt. Pepper's Lonely Hearts Club Band*. The album took 700 hours to record and included a 41-piece orchestra, barnyard noises, even a note that only dogs could hear. It was a phenomenal success and the last Beatles album produced with a shared vision. That vision was aided, it seemed, by LSD and marijuana, most notably in the controversial "Lucy in the Sky With Diamonds" and "A Day in the Life."

John acknowledged the musical departure represented by *Sgt. Pepper.* "The people who have bought our records in the past must realize that we couldn't go on making the same type [of music] forever," he said. "We must change, and I believe those people know this."

The Beatles had changed, and the times had changed with them —maybe even because of them. They would record more albums and turn out many more hits—"Hey Jude," the so-called White Album, *Abbey Road*—but under the weight of internal rivalries and business and personal pressures the group had begun to splinter. At one point John said, "I want a divorce." Finally, in 1970, the breakup was formalized when Paul announced he was going, and the Beatles let it be.

Amid a final spasm of Beatles hysteria—a wildfire rumor that Paul was dead—the group posed for one last photo session in August 1969.

The British Invasion

The Beatles' success touched off a hunt for the next hot British band. Soon Gerry and the Pacemakers, the Searchers, the Kinks, the Who, Freddie and the Dreamers, the Hollies, Herman's Hermits, and the Rolling Stones were feeding an American frenzy for British rock. Some groups moved away from the Beatles image to a grungier, darker outlook. Said Pete Townshend of the Who, "When I'm thirty I'm going to kill myself, 'cos I don't ever want to get old."

The Stones, with their energetic vulgarity and sexuality, caught on fast in Britain—their first album topped the charts in 1964. But they had a lackluster U.S. debut that same year, and it took their suggestive "(I Can't Get No) Satisfaction" in the summer of 1965 to grab young Americans. Their elders didn't necessarily go along: "After watching the Rolling Stones perform," said an Illinois newspaper, ". . . the Chicago stockyards smell good and clean by comparison."

Direct from ENGLAND
THE KINKS
in K-poi's
Royal Ball
DANCE WITH
The SPIRITS • TELSTARS • CASUALS • MOPTOPS
TUESDAY, JULY 6, 1965
H.I.C. Arena 7 - 11:30 p.m.
ALL SEATS $2.00 *Casual Dress*

The Rolling Stones display their bad-boy image in this "too many hands" pose.

James Brown, dubbed Soul Brother Number One, drops to his knees during a 1968 performance.

Aretha Franklin overcame stage fright by pretending she was at a party and was singing to friends.

You Gotta Have Soul

Soul music, in all its sad, bluesy, exuberant, gospel-based glory, sprang from the depths of the black experience in America. When Ray Charles *(inset)* shouted his trademark "What'd I say," listeners heard the spirited give-and-take between preacher and congregation that was at the heart of the music. Some listeners weren't pleased: Bluesman—and preacher—Big Bill Broonzy said, "He's mixing the blues and spirituals and I know that's wrong."

The most successful performers brought their own interpretation to soul—Wilson Pickett's sex-and-sweat-drenched "In the Midnight Hour," Percy Sledge's wrenching "When a Man Loves a Woman." But for pure heartrending plaintiveness, Otis Redding was the master. Redding could get his message across "in so few words," said his co-composer Steve Cropper, "that if you read them on paper they might not make any sense."

If Otis Redding stirred his audiences with soulful ballads, James Brown shook them up with raw, visceral vocals and dramatic showmanship. As the decade went on and the civil rights struggle empowered black Americans, Brown caught the feeling, recording in 1968 the rollicking anthem "Say It Loud—I'm Black and I'm Proud."

Aretha Franklin, a Baptist minister's daughter, cut her teeth on gospel hymns. Her smash-hit 1967 version of "Respect," a Redding composition, confirmed her as the Queen of Soul, and she swept through the rest of the decade with such top sellers as "A Natural Woman," "Chain of Fools," and "Since You've Been Gone." Franklin's life experiences, such as the death of her mother when she was 10, gave her singing its emotional power. "I might be just twenty-six," she told *Time* in 1968, "but I'm an old woman in disguise."

Otis Redding (right) squeezes out a soulful ballad. "He'd get right in front of you with that big fist up in the air," said a sideman, "and strut and sing that stuff until you were just foaming at the mouth."

*Psychedelic sounds—Iron Butterfly's distort-
ed guitar licks, Jefferson Airplane's powerful
rhythms, the violent poetry of the Doors, the
Dead's mix of blues, country, and rock.*

Acid Rock

San Francisco in the '60s was a hotbed of musical experimen-
tation under the sway of psychedelic drugs such as LSD, or
"acid." By 1966 the acid-rock era—heralded by the Beatles'
Rubber Soul album and the Byrds' "Eight Miles High"—was in full
flower. "Did I think 'Eight Miles High' was a drug song?" said the
Byrds' David Crosby. "No, I *knew* it was. We denied it, of course."

The first San Francisco acid band to make it nationally was Jefferson Airplane. Lead singer Grace Slick's icy, insistent vocals extolled the
virtues of turning on in such tunes as "White Rabbit," from the 1967

"Maybe if we play loud enough, we can shut out the world."

Jimi Hendrix

---

album *Surrealistic Pillow.* Drugs colored the music of the tripped-out
Grateful Dead, the darkly poetic Jim Morrison and the Doors, the
hard-rocking Iron Butterfly, and the endlessly creative Jimi Hendrix.

Janis Joplin was a coffeehouse singer turned rock messenger, her
sound raw and pure and razor sharp. Arriving in San Francisco from
Texas in 1966, she mined years of pain and rejection for a raucous,
profane, sexually charged blues style that brought her sudden fame
but little peace. She turned to alcohol and heroin for *Cheap Thrills*
(the name of her hit 1968 album with Big Brother and the Holding
Company), declaring, "I'd rather have 10 years of superhypermost
than live to be 70 by sitting in some goddamn chair watching TV."

What flies high may ultimately crash, and many of the acid-
rock stars landed hard   Hendrix, Joplin, and Morrison would
barely outlive the decade.

---

*Once described as a singer whose voice "has been aged in Southern Comfort,"
Janis Joplin had one rule: No cold beer before singing.*

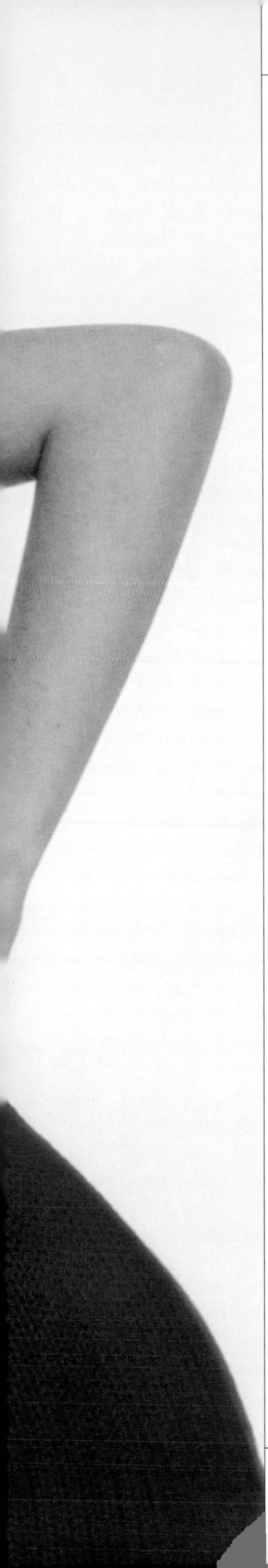

The Look of the 60s

★

DOING YOUR OWN THING

Boutique windows, art galleries, and home-decorating magazines all told the same story: Stately old standbys from the Lawson sofa to the little black dress were now old hat. The new aesthetic was, in the words of Pop artist Richard Hamilton, "popular, transient, expendable, low cost, mass produced, young, witty, sexy, glamorous, and Big Business."

The revolution in fashion was kicked off by the rebellious young, who, chameleon-like, would show their knees one day and get themselves up in romantic Gypsy outfits the next. In defiance of fashion's traditional gravity, the styles of exclusive designers were no longer trickling down to the masses. Instead, inspiration was trickling up from the kids. Savvy kid-watching British designer Mary Quant distilled what she saw on the streets into the irreverent, trim, youthful look called Mod. Its insignia was the miniskirt, and after 1964 it dominated fashion on both sides of the Atlantic.

Mod's simple geometry and bright colors echoed the canvases of Pop Art and cutting-edge furniture *(page 169),* and high fashion appropriated the illusions of Op Art *(page 171).* The counterculture made its own put-on, ragtag contributions to the look of the '60s *(pages 172-175),* summarizing the decade's aesthetic imperative: Do your own thing.

Lava lamp

Lesley Hornby, better known as Twiggy, is all angles and eyelashes in a Mod version of a schoolgirl's jumper. With her willowy, waifish look, the cockney teenager was the icon of '60s fashion.

Geometry Lessons

"Clothes are just not that important. They're not status symbols any longer. They're for fun."

Rudi Gernreich

A bathing suit featured in Vogue takes a novel approach to cleavage. Even more revealing was designer Rudi Gernreich's breast-baring suit. Stores that carried the suit drew irate picketers bearing signs that read WHAT NEXT? WE REBEL.

Soft, romantic alternatives to the hard-edged Mod look featured velvets, ribbons, and ruffles harking back to the early 19th century (right).

Psychedelic shirts, wide, gaudy ties, and lots of hair (left) proved the revolutionary proposition that men could have fun with fashion, too.

The bold design and vibrant colors of Robert Indiana's 1966 painting Love cropped up in many commercial items, including a Neiman Marcus department-store poster.

The comic-book look migrated to the nation's museums in Pop Art paintings such as Roy Lichtenstein's 1963 Drowning Girl.

Finnish designer Eero Aarnio's molded plastic Globe chair looks like something from the set of Star Trek. Globe radios and TVs echoed the chair's space-age look.

The flag turns fashionable (left), while Yves St. Laurent translates Dutch artist Piet Mondrian's rectangles into haute couture (below).

169

The sunglasses sported by the woman below are a lesson in Mod geometry. Instead of being hidden behind a placket, the oversize zipper of her stand-up collar is left in full view to double as an ornament.

London stylist Vidal Sassoon created the haircut at left to complement the sleek lines of Mary Quant's clothes. To fulfill the Sassoon ideal, absolutely straight hair was a must.

An armorplated Amazon wears an outfit created by Paris couturier Paco Rabanne for his 1967 Chain Mail collection. Fabricated of embossed steel squares alternating with smooth ones, the minidress, Rabanne suggested, would be ideal garb for "real James Bond girls."

In the hands of three Italian designers, a chair metamorphoses into a giant beanbag stuffed with polystyrene pellets (below). The "sacco"—Italian for sack—became a favorite of the hip.

Shunning the here and now, the model below plays at being a Gypsy queen. Boutiques were full of dress-up clothes that evoked the long ago or the far away. Men got in on the game, exchanging the Brooks Brothers uniform for a Nehru suit.

Photographed at a 1965 Op Art show at New York's Museum of Modern Art, a dress of oscillating chiffon and crepe by American couturier James Galanos mimics the kaleidoscopic effect of the Victor Vasarely collage in the background.

Anti-Fashion Fashion

Counterculturists frowned on commercial fashion design, but they evolved a distinctive style just the same. It tended to the dramatic: long, unstyled hair on both sexes and decorative facial hair on men spoke of a rejection of artifice, and work clothes like blue jeans of a rejection of middle-class values. The once sharp divide between male and female clothing was muffled by androgynous dressing, as displayed at a 1969 Rolling Stones concert, when Mick Jagger performed in an organdy frock.

Hippy chic gave an approving nod to the wild, swirling graphics and Day-Glo colors inspired by psychedelic imagery. Also in style were outfits assembled from attics and thrift shops and enhanced by the accouterments of non-Western cultures—Native American fringed vests, tunics from India, batik skirts from Indonesia.

Soon escaping the bounds of the youth culture, hippy chic flowed into establishment design *(previous pages)* and fed the profitable business of '60s style. As early as 1967, even Barbie dolls were sporting "Flower Power" outfits.

R. Crumb cartoon

As announced by the poster for the ultimate musical about the countercultural tribe *(left)*, the primary sign of hippiedom was hair. The style was flowing and natural, with optional beards and sideburns for men, and adornments ranging from earrings to bandannas to quirky hats *(below)*.

For young blacks *(left)*, hair became an important symbol of pride in race. They abandoned straighteners and relaxers for a natural look, using a special comb with long teeth to achieve the full-bodied Afro.

FEELIN' GROOVY

HIPPY POWER

this button is just an attempt to communicate

I AM A HUMAN BEING: DO NOT FOLD, SPINDLE OR MUTILATE

FREE ACID LICK HERE

The colorful buttons above literally turned countercultural dress into a mode of self-expression. The peace-symbol pendant also sent a message, and males and females alike adorned themselves with strings of love beads—preferably handmade.

From his wide-brimmed hat to his flag-draped toes, the man at near left is the epitome of anti-Establishment chic. Drab and underdressed in comparison, his companion wears the denim cutoffs that, like the granny glasses below, were seen everywhere.

Posters and an album cover for the British rock group Cream (below, center) show the counterculture's psychedelic style in full flower, with Art Nouveau-inspired swirls and vibrant fluorescent colors.

Custom-painted electric guitar

A tie-dye booth at the Woodstock Music and Art Fair in August 1969 offers shoppers a colorful array of wares. Countercultural fashion prized the one of a kind, the natural, and the homemade, and tie-dyeing—knotting fabric before dyeing it, preferably with natural dyes, to create sunburst patterns—satisfied on all counts.

The Race to the Moon

★

HITTING A KEYHOLE IN THE SKY

In a speech on May 25, 1961, President John F. Kennedy laid before his country a huge challenge: "I believe that this nation should commit itself to achieving the goal, before this decade is out, of landing a man on the moon and returning him safely to earth." They were brave words, for the United States lagged far behind the Soviet Union in the race to conquer space, as it had ever since the Soviets' orbiting *Sputnik I* stunned the world in 1957. Three weeks before the president's speech, America's Project Mercury manned-flight program had put its first astronaut into space, when Alan Shepard made a short suborbital flight. However, that achievement was overshadowed by cosmonaut Yuri Gagarin's Earth-circling flight a month earlier. Kennedy thought it might take $20 billion to compete in space. "While we cannot guarantee that we shall one day be first," he said, "we can guarantee that any failure to make this effort will make us last."

Nine months would pass before astronaut John Glenn would ride a rocket 160 miles up into the great new ocean of space *(inset)*. On February 20, 1962, he would achieve orbit, pilot his capsule three times around the Earth, and after four hours and 55 minutes, come blazing safely home again. By then, the Soviets had put up a cosmonaut for more than 24 hours. But the United States was on its way.

Suited up and raring to go, John Glenn had a test pilot's appreciation of the physics of his mission. Achieving orbit, he said, required tremendous accuracy and would be like "hitting a keyhole in the sky."

Proof Positive

"I'm doing great. It's fun. I'm not coming in."

Ed White, *Gemini 4*

What you'd like to be able to do," grinned astronaut Gus Grissom, "is just kick the tires and go." In time, NASA planners would make space travel seem almost routine. Yet in 1965, they did not know if a weightless human body could function for the week or more it would take to reach the Moon and return. Or if astronauts could perform essential tasks in space outside the capsule. Or, most important, if they could fly their spacecraft through the complex rendezvous and docking maneuvers required for a Moon landing. Project Gemini (so named for its two-man crews) would address those questions with 10 flights between March 1965 and November 1966.

Grissom, who was so involved in the development of NASA's new space capsule that workers at the McDonnell Aircraft plant dubbed it the Gusmobile, was first aloft in *Gemini 3* (*1* and *2* were unmanned tests). He and John Young shifted the capsule into varying orbits by means of 16 small rocket thrusters. *Gemini 4* that June saw the first American spacewalk when Ed White spent 20 minutes outside on the end of a 24-foot umbilical. But the Soviets were still

Ed White floats in space at the end of a gold-plated umbilical that provided oxygen and communication with command pilot Jim McDivitt in the capsule. White holds a compressed-air "zip gun" to help him maneuver. Attached to the gun is a 35-mm camera, and on his chest is a 12-minute emergency oxygen supply.

Gemini 7 orbits aft end forward in this photo, taken by astronaut Tom Stafford from Gemini 6. The two spacecraft kept company 183 miles above the Earth for more than five hours and at one point closed to within a foot of each other.

After splashdown 14 miles from a waiting aircraft carrier, Gemini 6 astronauts Tom Stafford (left) and Wally Schirra prepare to leave their craft while navy frogmen, having attached a flotation collar, phone back that all's well.

ahead, having made their own space-walk nearly three months before.

Russian cosmonauts had not, however, achieved a manned space rendezvous when *Gemini 6* lifted off on December 12, 1965, with astronauts Wally Schirra and Thomas Stafford aboard. Their mission: to rendezvous with *Gemini 7,* which had been orbiting for 11 days and was 1,245 miles ahead. In less than six hours *Gemini 6* caught up, and for three orbits the pair flew in close formation. Rendezvous accomplished, *Gemini 6* returned home, and *Gemini 7* went on to set a record of almost 14 days in space, with no ill effects for astronauts Frank Borman and James Lovell.

Neil Armstrong and David Scott chalked up another success on March 16, 1966, when they docked *Gemini 8* with an unmanned vehicle. But there were still critical kinks to be worked out, since astronauts reported fatigue after a spacewalk and said that their umbilicals got in the way. With *Gemini 12,* the worst of these problems were solved. Equipped with a shorter umbilical, a special harness, and Velcro handholds, Edwin "Buzz" Aldrin worked 129 minutes in space without fatigue. The answers to NASA's questions were all affirmative. On to the Moon.

Gemini patches

Apollo: Disaster and Triumph

Time magazine memorializes the Apollo 1 astronauts, shown in front of the spacecraft's launch pad. They died the week before when a flash fire engulfed the command module's interior (below) during a preflight test.

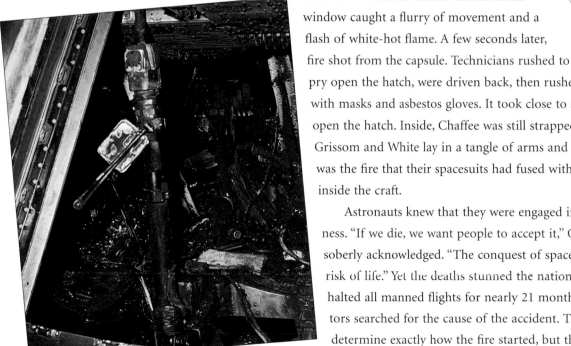

Apollo patch

The third and final act in the great drama began with tragedy. On Friday afternoon, January 27, 1967, three astronauts sat strapped into their *Apollo 1* spacecraft atop a Saturn rocket at Florida's John F. Kennedy Space Center. *Apollo 1*'s crew consisted of *Gemini* veterans Gus Grissom and Ed White and rookie Roger Chaffee, at 31 the youngest member of the astronaut corps picked to go into space. In three weeks they would take *Apollo* into Earth orbit. Now they were performing a launch simulation—the craft pressurized, the pilots breathing pure oxygen while they ran through the lengthy drill.

At 6:31 p.m. a voice, probably Chaffee's, came over the intercom: "Fire. I smell fire." Then more insistently: "Fire aboard the spacecraft!" A TV camera trained on the hatch window caught a flurry of movement and a flash of white-hot flame. A few seconds later, fire shot from the capsule. Technicians rushed to pry open the hatch, were driven back, then rushed forward again with masks and asbestos gloves. It took close to six minutes to open the hatch. Inside, Chaffee was still strapped to his seat. Grissom and White lay in a tangle of arms and legs. So intense was the fire that their spacesuits had fused with molten nylon inside the craft.

Astronauts knew that they were engaged in a risky business. "If we die, we want people to accept it," Grissom once soberly acknowledged. "The conquest of space is worth the risk of life." Yet the deaths stunned the nation, and NASA halted all manned flights for nearly 21 months as investigators searched for the cause of the accident. They did not determine exactly how the fire started, but they found problems that contributed to the disaster. Engineers set to work correct-

Camera in hand, Dave Scott stands in the hatch of Apollo 9's command module as it passes over the Mississippi Valley. Fellow astronaut Rusty Schweickart took the picture.

ing the flaws, rerouting wiring, discarding flammable materials, re-designing the hatch, changing procedures, and testing and retesting the huge, immensely complex spacecraft.

Veteran Wally Schirra and two freshman astronauts were aboard when *Apollo 7,* the first manned flight after the disaster, went into orbit on October 11, 1968. All systems were go, and the pace of space shots accelerated quickly. Lifted into space by a gigantic Saturn V booster rocket in late December, *Apollo 8* astronauts Frank Borman, Jim Lovell, and William Anders became the first men to circle the Moon and return to Earth.

Apollo 9's mission the following March was the trickiest, most critical yet: a test of the fragile-looking lunar landing module stowed with its legs folded in the nose of the Saturn booster. In Earth orbit, Jim McDivitt, Dave Scott, and Russell Schweickart separated the command module from the booster, then plucked the lunar lander from the booster's nose. On the mission's fifth day, McDivitt and Schweickart entered Spider, as they called their lander, undocked from the command craft, and maneuvered independently for six hours, sometimes as far as 100 miles from the mother ship. Radioed a jubilant Scott as they returned, "You're the biggest, friendliest, funniest-looking spider I've ever seen." The spider docked without a hitch.

"What a ride! What a ride!"

Gene Cernan, *Apollo 10*

Only the dress rehearsal remained. On May 18 Tom Stafford, John Young, and Gene Cernan in *Apollo 10* did everything except touch down on the lunar surface. While Young orbited 69 miles above the Moon in the command module, nicknamed Charlie Brown, Stafford and Cernan took their lander Snoopy down to within 47,500 feet of the Moon. "We're right there! We're right over it!" Cernan exclaimed to Mission Control. "I'm telling you, we are low! We're close, babe! This is it!"

Earth appears to rise over the Moon in the sequence above, taken by the Apollo 10 astronauts as they circled the Moon. They captured the scene at right as they streaked home later. The Baja California peninsula is visible between clouds at center.

> "That's one small step for man, one giant leap for mankind."

Neil Armstrong, *Apollo 11*
July 20, 1969

Buzz Aldrin clambers slowly down Eagle's ladder to join Neil Armstrong on the surface of the Moon.

Mission Accomplished

Neil Armstrong, *Apollo 11* commander, was flying the lunar lander manually, easing it down onto the Sea of Tranquillity. (The auto targeter had been directing *Eagle* into a rocky crater, so Armstrong took over.) Back across 240,000 miles to Mission Control in Houston came the calm voice of his copilot, Buzz Aldrin: "Seventy-five feet . . . six forward . . . light's on . . . down two and a half . . . 40 feet . . . picking up some dust . . . 30 feet . . . drifting to the right a little . . . contact light . . . okay. Engine stop." A pause, then Armstrong said, "Houston, Tranquillity Base here. The *Eagle* has landed!"

With those historic words at 4:17:41 p.m. EDT on July 20, 1969, the *Apollo 11* astronauts—Armstrong, Aldrin, and Michael Collins—did more than meet John F. Kennedy's challenge of eight years before, and far more than surpass the Soviets in space. They launched humankind on a new era of exploration, on a journey through the universe from which it would not turn back.

The mission itself, televised back to half a billion earthlings, was picture perfect. First Armstrong, then Aldrin walked on the surface of the Moon. They erected an American flag, collected about 48 pounds of rocks, and set up scientific experiments. Then, after two hours and 31 minutes, they returned to *Eagle* to rest before kicking in the ascent stage (its thrust knocked the flag flat) and rejoining Collins in the orbiting command module for the long ride home.

The astronauts left behind their footprints and *Eagle*'s descent stage. Affixed to one of the legs was a plaque bearing the date, the signatures of the astronauts and President Richard Nixon, and the legend "We came in peace."

Buzz Aldrin makes a footprint in moon dust. He took the photograph with a 70-mm Hasselblad camera that he and Armstrong left behind to save weight.

ACKNOWLEDGMENTS

The editors wish to thank the following individuals and institutions for their valuable assistance in the preparation of this volume:
James Beck, A.J.'s Sport Stop, Vienna, Va.; Jeff Doranz, Jeff's Baseball Corner & The Time Machine, Springfield, Va.; Mike Gentry, NASA Media Services, Houston, Tex.; Cyndy Gilley, Do You Graphics, Woodbine, Md.; Allan Goodrich, John F. Kennedy Library, Boston; Erin Hogan, Rock and Roll Hall of Fame and Museum, Cleveland, Ohio; Mary Ison and staff, Library of Congress, Washington, D.C.; Elliott Landy, Woodstock, N.Y.; Hank Thompson, Raleigh, N.C.; Robert L. White, The Kennedy Collection, Catonsville, Md.

BIBLIOGRAPHY

BOOKS

American Decades: 1960-1969. Ed. by Richard Layman. Detroit: Gale Research, 1995.

Anderson, Terry H. *The Movement and the Sixties.* New York: Oxford University Press, 1995.

Barnard, Stephen. *Rock.* New York: Schirmer Books, 1986.

The Beatles: From Yesterday to Today. Boston: Bulfinch Press, 1996.

Beschloss, Michael R. *The Crisis Years: Kennedy and Khrushchev, 1960-1963.* New York: Edward Burlingame Books, 1991.

The Best of Sports Illustrated. New York: Sports Illustrated, 1996.

Branch, Taylor. *Parting the Waters.* New York: Simon and Schuster, 1988.

Briggs, Jennifer (comp.). *Strive to Excel: The Will and Wisdom of Vince Lombardi.* Nashville: Rutledge Hill Press, 1997.

Brode, Douglas. *The Films of the Sixties.* Secaucus, N.J.: Citadel Press, 1980.

Castleman, Harry, and Walter J. Podrazik. *Watching TV: Four Decades of American Television.* New York: McGraw-Hill, 1982.

Clayson, Alan. *Beat Merchants.* London: Blandford, 1996.

Cox, Stephen. *The Addams Chronicles.* New York: HarperPerennial, 1991.

Crothers, Tim. *Greatest Teams.* New York: Sports Illustrated, 1998.

Crumb, R. *The R. Crumb Coffee Table Art Book.* Ed. by Peter Poplaski. Boston: Little, Brown, 1997.

Daniels, George G. *The XIX Olympiad: Mexico City 1968, Sapporo 1972.* Los Angeles: World Sport Research & Publications, 1996.

Davidson, James West, et al. *Nation of Nations: A Narrative History of the American Republic* (2nd ed.). New York: McGraw-Hill, 1994.

Davies, Hunter. *The Beatles.* New York: McGraw-Hill, 1978.

Dougan, Clark, Samuel Lipsman, and the Editors of Boston Publishing Company. *A Nation Divided* (The Vietnam Experience series). Boston: Boston Publishing, 1984.

Dougan, Clark, Stephen Weiss, and the Editors of Boston Publishing Company:
    The American Experience in Vietnam. New York: W. W. Norton, 1988.
    Nineteen Sixty-Eight (The Vietnam Experience series). Boston: Boston Publishing, 1983.

Encyclopedia of the Vietnam War. Ed. by Stanley I. Kutler. New York: Macmillan Library, 1996.

Fischer, Julene. *Images of War* (The Vietnam Experience series). Boston: Boston Publishing, 1986.

Friedan, Betty. *The Feminine Mystique.* New York: W. W. Norton, 1963.

Garrow, David J. *Bearing the Cross.* New York: Vintage Books, 1988.

Gitlin, Todd. *The Sixties.* New York: Bantam Books, 1993.

Gordon, Lois G., and Alan Gordon:
    American Chronicle. New York: Atheneum, 1987.
    The Columbia Chronicles of American Life: 1910-1992. New York: Columbia University Press, 1995.

Greatest Football Games of All Time. New York: Sports Illustrated, 1997.

Haining, Peter. *Raquel Welch.* New York: St. Martin's Press, 1984.

Halstead, Fred. *Out Now!* New York: Monad Press, 1978.

Hauser, Thomas. *Muhammad Ali.* New York: Simon and Schuster, 1991.

Hyams, Jay. *The Life and Times of the Western Movie.* New York: Gallery Books, 1983.

I Want to Take You Higher: The Psychedelic Era, 1965-1969. Ed. by James Henke. San Francisco: Chronicle Books, 1997.

Karnow, Stanley. *Vietnam: A History.* New York: Viking Press, 1983.

Kasher, Steven. *The Civil Rights Movement.* New York: Abbeville Press, 1996.

Katz, Ephraim. *The Film Encyclopedia.* New York: Thomas Y. Crowell, 1979.

Kerrod, Robin. *The Illustrated History of NASA.* London: Multimedia, 1986.

Kesey's Garage Sale. New York: Viking Press, 1973.

Klatell, David A., and Norman Marcus. *Sports for Sale: Television, Money, and the Fans.* New York: Oxford University Press, 1988.

Kleinfelder, Rita Lang. *When We Were Young: A Baby-Boomer Yearbook.* New York: Prentice Hall, 1993.

Kramer, Daniel. *Bob Dylan.* New York: Citadel Underground, 1991.

Landy, Elliott. *Woodstock Vision.* New York: Continuum, 1994.

Leifer, Eric M. *Making the Majors: The Transformation of Team Sports in America.* Cambridge, Mass.: Harvard University Press, 1995.

Lens, Sidney. *Vietnam.* New York: Lodestar Books, 1990.

Life—the 60's. Ed. by Doris C. O'Neil. Boston: Bulfinch Press, 1989.

Life in Camelot: The Kennedy Years. Ed. by Philip B. Kunhardt Jr. Boston: Little, Brown, 1988.

Life in Space. Alexandria, Va.: Time-Life Books, 1983.

Lobenthal, Joel. *Radical Rags.* New York: Abbeville Press, 1990.

McAleer, Dave. *The Fab British Rock 'n' Roll Invasion of 1964.* New York: St. Martin's Press, 1994.

McCarry, Charles. *Citizen Nader.* New York: Saturday Review Press, 1972.

MacPherson, Myra. *Long Time Passing.* New York: Anchor Books, 1984.

Malcolm X. *The Autobiography of Malcolm X.* New York: Ballantine Books, 1973.

Manchester, William. *One Brief Shining Moment.* Boston: Little, Brown, 1983.

Martin Luther King, Jr. New York: W. W. Norton, 1976.

Mayer, Robert N. *The Consumer Movement.* Boston: Twayne Publishers, 1989.

Mead, William B. *The Explosive Sixties.* Alexandria, Va. Redefinition, 1989.

Miller, James. *"Democracy Is in the Streets": From Port Huron to the Siege of Chicago.* New York: Simon and Schuster, 1987.

Morgan, Edward P. *The 60s Experience: Hard Lessons About Modern America.* Philadelphia: Temple University Press, 1991.

Nader, Ralph. *Unsafe at Any Speed: The Designed-In Dangers of the American Automobile.* New York: Grossman Publishers, 1965.

The New York Times Book of Sports Legends. Ed. by Joseph J. Vecchione. New York: Times Books, 1991.

Norman, Philip. *Shout!* New York: Simon and Schuster, 1981.

Oates, Stephen B. *Let the Trumpet Sound.* New York: Harper & Row, 1982.

Ochs, Michael. *1000 Record Covers.* London: Taschen, 1996.

O'Neill, William L. *Coming Apart.* Chicago: Quadrangle Books, 1971.

Our Glorious Century. Pleasantville, N.Y.: Reader's Digest, 1994.

Our Times. Atlanta: Turner Publishing, 1995.

Ovenden, Kevin. *Malcolm X: Socialism and Black Nationalism.* London: Bookmarks, 1992.

Palmer, Robert. *Rock and Roll.* New York: Harmony Books, 1995.

Patterson, James T. *Grand Expectations: The United States, 1945-1974.* New York: Oxford University Press, 1996.

Peary, Danny. *Cult Movies 3.* New York: Simon and Schuster, 1988.

Pfeiffer, Lee, and Philip Lisa. *The Incredible World of 007.* New York: Citadel Press, 1995.

Phillips, Gene D. *Stanley Kubrick.* New York: Popular Library, 1975.

Phillips, Louis, and Burnham Holmes. *The TV Almanac.* New York: Macmillan, 1994.

Ralbovsky, Marty. *Super Bowl.* New York: Hawthorn Books, 1971.

Ratcliff, Carter. *Andy Warhol.* New York: Abbeville Press, 1983.

Rees, Dafydd, and Luke Crampton. *Encyclopedia of Rock Stars.* New York: DK Publishing, 1996.

The Rolling Stone Illustrated History of Rock and Roll. Ed. by Anthony DeCurtis and James Henke. New York: Random House, 1992.

Sackett, Susan. *The Reporter Book of Box Office Hits.* New York: Billboard Books, 1996.

Schlesinger, Arthur M., Jr. *A Thousand Days: John F. Kennedy in the White House.* Boston: Houghton Mifflin, 1965.

Second to None: A Documentary History of American Women. Ed. by Ruth Barnes Moynihan, Cynthia Russett, and Laurie Crumpacker. Lincoln: University of Nebraska Press, 1993.

Settel, Irving. *A Pictorial History of Television* (2nd ed.). New York: Frederick Ungar, 1983.

Siddons, Larry. *The Olympics at 100.* New York: Macmillan, 1995.

Siegel, Scott, and Barbara Siegel. *The Encyclopedia of Hollywood.* New York: Avon Books, 1990.

Stark, Steven D. *Glued to the Set.* New York: Free Press, 1997.

Stern, Jane. *Sixties People.* New York: Alfred A. Knopf, 1990.

Stevens, Jay. *Storming Heaven: LSD and the American Dream.* New York: Atlantic Monthly Press, 1987.

The Story of Rock 'n' Roll: The Year-by-Year Illustrated Chronicle. Miami, Fla.: Carlton, 1995.

Trétiack, Philippe. *Andy Warhol.* New York: Universe, 1997.

Truffaut, François. *Hitchcock.* New York: Simon and Schuster, 1966.

Van Deburg, William L. *Black Camelot: African-American Culture Heroes in Their Times, 1960-1980.* Chicago: University of Chicago Press, 1997.

Viorst, Milton. *Fire in the Streets: America in the 1960s.* New York: Simon and Schuster, 1979.

Ward, Geoffrey C. *Baseball: An Illustrated History.* New York: Alfred A. Knopf, 1994.

The Way We Were. Ed. by Robert MacNeil. New York: Carroll & Graf Publishers, 1988.

Weisbrot, Robert. *Freedom Bound: A History of America's Civil Rights Movement.* New York: Plume, 1990.

Weiss, Ann E. *Money Games: The Business of Sports.* Boston: Houghton Mifflin, 1993.

Wexler, Sanford:
   The Civil Rights Movement. New York: Facts On File, 1993.
   The Vietnam War. New York: Facts On File, 1992.

Wiener, Allen J. (comp.). *The Beatles: A Recording History.* Jefferson, N.C.: McFarland, 1986.

Williams, Juan. *Eyes on the Prize: America's Civil Rights Years, 1954-1965.* New York: Penguin, 1987.

Winship, Michael. *Television.* New York: Random House, 1988.

Wolfe, Tom. *The Electric Kool-Aid Acid Test.* New York: Bantam Books, 1969.

Wolff, Miles. *Lunch at the 5 and 10* (rev. ed.). Chicago: I. R. Dee, 1990.

Yablonsky, Lewis. *The Hippie Trip.* New York: Pegasus, 1968.

Zaroulis, Nancy, and Gerald Sullivan. *Who Spoke Up?: American Protest Against the War in Vietnam, 1963-1975.* Garden City, N.Y.: Doubleday, 1984.

Zmijewsky, Boris, and Lee Pfeiffer. *The Films of Clint Eastwood.* Secaucus, N.J.: Citadel Press, 1990.

PERIODICALS

American Heritage, June/July 1982.

Howe, Desson. "James Bond, Agent of Change." *Washington Post,* December 21, 1997.

Life, January 1960-December 1969.

Time, July 1961-December 1967.

OTHER SOURCES

"THE ALT.MOVIES.KUBRICK FAQ" Available: http://www.krusch.com/kubrick/faq.html. March 20, 1998.

First Ladies. Available: http:www.whitehouse.gov/WH/glimpse/firstladies/html/JK35.html

U.S. Human Space Flights. Available: http:www.hq.nasa.gov/osf/flights.html

INDEX

Numerals in italics indicate an illustration of the subject mentioned.

TIME® LIFE BOOKS

Time-Life Books is a division of Time Life Inc.

TIME LIFE INC.
PRESIDENT and CEO: George Artandi

TIME-LIFE BOOKS
PUBLISHER/MANAGING EDITOR: Neil Kagan
VICE PRESIDENT, MARKETING: Joseph A. Kuna

OUR AMERICAN CENTURY
Turbulent Years: The 60s

EDITORS: Sarah Brash, Loretta Britten
DIRECTOR, NEW PRODUCT DEVELOPMENT:
Elizabeth D. Ward
DIRECTOR OF MARKETING: Pamela R. Farrell

Deputy Editors: Roxie France-Nuriddin, Kristin Hanneman
(principals), Charles J. Hagner
Associate Editor/Research and Writing: Gemma Slack
Marketing Manager: Janine Wilkin
Assistant Product Manager: Terri Miller
Picture Associate: Anne Whittle
Senior Copyeditor: Anne Farr
Technical Art Specialist: John Drummond
Picture Coordinator: Betty H. Weatherley
Editorial Assistant: Christine Higgins

Design for **Our American Century** by Antonio Alcalá,
Studio A, Alexandria, Virginia.

Special Contributors: Maggie Debelius, Paul Mathless (editing
and writing); Ronald H. Bailey, Linda Bellamy, Janet Cave,
George Daniels, Laura Foreman, Glenn McNatt, Ellen Phillips
(writing); Ann-Louise Gates, Ruth Goldberg, Mimi Harrison,
Terrell Smith, Anastasia Warpinski (research); Kimberly
Grandcolas (production); Richard Friend, Christina Hagopian
(design); Susan Nedrow (index).

Correspondents: Christine Hinze (London), Christina
Lieberman (New York), Maria Vincenza Aloisi (Paris).

Director of Finance: Christopher Hearing
Directors of Book Production: Marjann Caldwell, Patricia Pascale
Director of Publishing Technology: Betsi McGrath
Director of Photography and Research: John Conrad Weiser
Director of Editorial Administration: Barbara Levitt
Production Manager: Virginia Reardon
Quality Assurance Manager: James King
Chief Librarian: Louise D. Forstall

EDITORIAL CONSULTANT
Richard B. Stolley is currently senior editorial adviser at Time
Inc. After 19 years at *Life* magazine as a reporter, bureau chief,
and assistant managing editor, he became the first managing
editor of *People* magazine, a position he held with great success
for eight years. He then returned to *Life* magazine as managing
editor and later served as editorial director for all Time Inc.
magazines. In 1997 Stolley received the Henry Johnson Fisher
Award for Lifetime Achievement, the magazine industry's
highest honor.

Library of Congress Cataloging-in-Publication Data
Turbulent years: the 60s / by the editors of Time-Life Books.
p. cm.—(Our American century)
Includes bibliographical references and index.
ISBN 0-7835-5503-2
1. United States—History—1961–1969
2. United States—History—1961–1969—Pictorial works.
I. Time-Life Books.   II. Series.
E841.T78 1998
973.923—dc21   98-18527
                                                          CIP

Text Credit:

Page 38: From *The Feminine Mystique* by Betty Friedan.
Copyright © 1983, 1974, 1973, 1963 by Betty Friedan.
Reprinted by permission of W. W. Norton & Company, Inc.

Other History Publications:

World War II
What Life Was Like
The American Story
Voices of the Civil War
The American Indians
Lost Civilizations
Mysteries of the Unknown
Time Frame
The Civil War
Cultural Atlas

For information on and a full description of any of the Time-
Life Books series listed above, please call 1-800-621-7026
or write:

Reader Information
Time-Life Customer Service
P.O. Box C-32068
Richmond, Virginia 23261-2068